PROBATE LAW

by
Margaret C. Jasper

Oceana's Legal Almanac Series:
Law for the Layperson

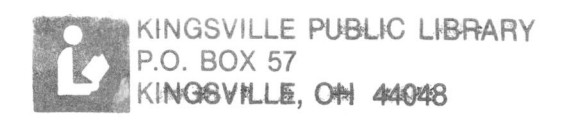

1997
Oceana Publications, Inc.
Dobbs Ferry, N.Y.

Information contained in this work has been obtained by Oceana Publications from sources believed to be reliable. However, neither the Publisher nor its authors guarantee the accuracy or completeness of any information published herein, and neither Oceana nor its authors shall be responsible for any errors, omissions or damages arising from the use of this information. This work is published with the understanding that Oceana and its authors are supplying information, but are not attempting to render legal or other professional services. If such services are required, the assistance of an appropriate professional should be sought.

You may order this or any other Oceana publications by visiting Oceana's Web Site at http://www.oceanalaw.com

---

ISBN: 0-379-11239-6 (alk. paper)

Oceana's Legal Almanac Series: Law for the Layperson
ISSN: 1075-7376

© 1997 by Oceana Publications, Inc.

All rights reserved. No part of this publication may be reproduced or transmitted in any form or by any means, electronic or mechanical, including photocopy, recording, xerography, or any information storage and retrieval system, without permission in writing from the publisher.

Manufactured in the United States of America on acid-free paper.

To My Husband Chris

**Your love and support
are my motivation and inspiration**

and

In memory of my son, Jimmy

ABOUT THE AUTHOR

MARGARET C. JASPER is an attorney engaged in the general practice of law in South Salem, New York, concentrating in the areas of personal injury and entertainment law. Ms. Jasper holds a Juris Doctor degree from Pace University School of Law, White Plains, New York, is a member of the New York and Connecticut bars, and is certified to practice before the United States District Courts for the Southern and Eastern Districts of New York, and the United States Supreme Court.

Ms. Jasper has been appointed to the panel of arbitrators of the American Arbitration Association and the law guardian panel for the Family Court of the State of New York, and is a New York State licensed real estate broker and member of the Westchester County Board of Realtors, operating as Jasper Real Estate, in South Salem, New York.

Ms. Jasper is the author and general editor of the following legal almanacs: Juvenile Justice and Children's Law; Marriage and Divorce; Estate Planning; The Law of Contracts; The Law of Dispute Resolution; Law for the Small Business Owner; The Law of Personal Injury; Real Estate Law for the Homeowner and Broker; Everyday Legal Forms; Dictionary of Selected Legal Terms; The Law of Medical Malpractice; The Law of Product Liability; The Law of No-Fault Insurance; The Law of Immigration; The Law of Libel and Slander; The Law of Buying and Selling; Elder Law; The Right to Die; AIDS Law; Obscenity, Pornography and the Law; The Law of Child Custody; The Law of Debt Collection; Consumer Rights Law; and Bankruptcy Law for the Individual Debtor.

TABLE OF CONTENTS

INTRODUCTION xi
CHAPTER 1: HISTORICAL BACKGROUND 1
CHAPTER 2: WILLS 3
    In General 3
    Locating the Will 3
    Proving the Will 4
    Disinheritance 4
    Contesting the Will 5
CHAPTER 3: INTESTACY 7
    In General 7
    Procedure 7
CHAPTER 4: THE PERSONAL REPRESENTATIVE 9
    In General 9
    Responsibilities of the Personal Representative 9
        Opening the Estate 10
        Notification 10
        Estate Accounts 11
CHAPTER 5: ADMINISTERING THE ESTATE 13
    In General 13
    Supervised Administration 13
    Unsupervised Administration 13
    Small Estate Administration 14
        Administration by Court Order 14
        Administration by Affidavit 15
    Ancillary Administration 15
CHAPTER 6: INVENTORY 17
    In General 17
    Locating Assets of the Estate 17
    Appraising the Assets 19
    Final Inventory and Appraisal 19
CHAPTER 7: DEBTS 21
    In General 21
    Payment of Claims 21
    Real Property 21

- CHAPTER 8: TRANSFERRING PROPERTY 23
  - In General 23
    - Jointly Owned Property 23
    - Community Property States 24
  - Life Insurance and Pension Plan Proceeds 24
- CHAPTER 9: TAXATION 25
  - In General 25
  - Types of Tax Returns 25
    - Income Tax 25
      - Decedent's Personal Income Tax 25
      - Estate Income Tax 25
    - Estate Tax 26
      - The Federal Estate Tax 26
      - State Inheritance and Estate Tax 26
- CHAPTER 10: FEES 27
  - In General 27
  - The Personal Representative 27
  - The Estate Lawyer 27
  - Fee Limitations and Arrangements 27
  - Fee Reduction 28
- CHAPTER 11: CLOSING THE ESTATE 29
  - In General 29
  - The Final Accounting 29
    - Assets 29
    - Expenses 29
    - Taxes 29
    - Balance of Estate 29
  - The Supervised Estate 30
    - Court Petition 30
    - Sworn Statement 30
- CHAPTER 12: ASSET DISTRIBUTION 31
  - In General 31
  - Beneficiaries 31
  - Survivorship Periods 31
  - Distribution in Kind 31
  - Intestate Distribution 32

Minors	32
Appointing a Guardian for Minor Children	32
CHAPTER 13: THE UNIFORM PROBATE CODE	**35**
In General	35
Overview of the Uniform Probate Code	35
Article I - General Provisions	35
Article II - Intestate Succession and Wills	35
Article III - Probate of Wills and Administration	35
Article IV - Foreign Personal Representatives -Ancillary Administration	36
Article V - Protection of Persons Under Disability and Their Property	36
Article VI - Non-Probate Transfers	36
Article VII - Trust Administration	36
Article VIII - Effective Date and Repealer	36
CHAPTER 14: PROBATE AVOIDANCE	**37**
In General	37
Probate Exemptions	37
Jointly Owned Property	37
Trusts	38
In General	38
The Irrevocable Trust	38
The Revocable Living Trust	39
Marital Living Trust	39
Childrens Trust	40
Spendthrift Trust	40
Informal Probate Avoidance	40
APPENDICES	**41**
APPENDIX 1 - SAMPLE WILL	43
APPENDIX 2 - SAMPLE CODICIL TO WILL	47
APPENDIX 3 - SELF-PROVING AFFIDAVIT	49
APPENDIX 4 - SAMPLE DEPOSITION OF WITNESS	51
APPENDIX 5 - STATE RULES OF INHERITANCE	53
APPENDIX 6 - SAMPLE PROBATE PETITION	63
APPENDIX 7 - SAMPLE NOTICE OF PROBATE	67

APPENDIX 8 - SAMPLE COURT ORDER ISSUING
    LETTERS TESTAMENTARY 69
APPENDIX 9 - STATE LAW EXCEPTIONS TO
    CONVENTIONAL PROBATE 71
APPENDIX 10 - SAMPLE NEW YORK STATE
    SUCCESSION TAX RETURN 77
APPENDIX 11 - UNIFORM PROBATE CODE TABLE OF
    CONTENTS 91
GLOSSARY 107
BIBLIOGRAPHY AND SUGGESTED READING 115

INTRODUCTION

Most people, at some point in their life, experience the loss of a loved one. Family members and friends are usually left with the task of settling that person's affairs. If the decedent left a will, his or her last wishes pertaining to the distribution of his or her assets must be carried out according to its terms.

This responsibility is borne by the person named in the will as the decedent's personal representative. The decedent may have chosen a friend or relative to act as his or her personal representative. Sometimes the attorney who drafted the will is named as the personal representative. Often, a bank or trust corporation will act as the personal representative of an estate, particularly a large estate with a number of complex assets.

If the decedent did not leave a will—*i.e.*, died intestate—the administration of the estate will take place according to the law of the state in which the decedent resided. In the case of intestacy, the court appoints an individual to act as the personal representative responsible for administering the estate. Sometimes the family members are permitted to elect a personal representative.

The term probate literally means "to prove." The technical meaning refers to the process of proving the validity of a will before a court. However, as commonly used, the term probate refers to the administration of a decedent's estate under judicial supervision, even if the decedent died intestate.

This almanac presents a general discussion of probate law, and an overview of the procedures involved. The goal is to provide the reader with a basic understanding of the system and what one may expect if called upon to participate, either as a personal representative or other interested party. The almanac further discusses common probate avoidance devices, such as trusts, which may be used to simplify the distribution of one's estate without unnecessary court involvement and delay.

Because uniformity has not yet been achieved among the states, the reader is advised to check the laws of his or her own jurisdiction pertaining to specific questions on probate law and procedure.

The Appendix provides sample forms, applicable statutes, and other pertinent information and data. The Glossary contains definitions of many of the terms used throughout the almanac.

CHAPTER 1:

HISTORICAL BACKGROUND

Probate is the process by which a will is determined by a court to fulfill the legal requirements set forth by the state. The probate process has its roots in medieval English history. At that time, ownership of land meant wealth and power, and the transfer of land upon the death of the owner required the direct involvement of the king's courts. Personal property, however, was of little concern to the king and was transferred by simpler means.

After independence was won, the American colonies retained the English common-law procedure, but ceased to distinguish between the disposition of real and personal property, instead requiring judicial proceedings to dispose of all property upon death.

The probate process under modern-day English law has been streamlined and currently surpasses the system in place in America today. In fact, the drafters of the Uniform Probate Code (UPC) relied on many of the modern rules and procedures existing under English law in drafting the UPC, which gained approval in 1969.

There is much public dissatisfaction with the current American probate system. It is perceived to be a lengthy procedure rampant with fraud and greed. There is little uniformity among the states, although the UPC has provided a framework from which the states can work towards uniformity. Nevertheless, the majority of states have not adopted the UPC in its entirety, although many states have adopted portions of the law, or have enacted their own legislation patterned after UPC provisions.

In response to their aversion to the probate process, many individuals have moved towards avoiding probate altogether, using any number of probate avoidance methods in planning their estate.

CHAPTER 2:

WILLS

In General

The first step in the probate process is determining whether the decedent left a valid will. A will is the legal declaration of a person's wishes for the disposition of his or her possessions after death. The will provides for the distribution of the decedent's property to certain individuals, in the manner and proportion the decedent designated.

The will also designates a personal representative—the person responsible for administering the decedent's estate—also commonly referred to as the executor (masculine) or executrix (feminine). The role of the personal representative is further discussed in Chapter 4 of this Almanac.

A sample will of a married woman with minor children is set forth in the Appendix.

If the decedent died without a will—that is, *intestate*—his or her property will generally be distributed to the decedent's family members according to state law. The law of intestacy is further discussed in Chapter 3.

Locating the Will

It is important that the decedent's will be located as soon as possible. The will must be submitted to the court where the decedent legally resided within a certain time period after death. Until the will is found, if one exists, the family should designate someone, such as a family member, to act as personal representative in the interim.

The acting personal representative is responsible for determining whether a valid will exists. The decedent's personal files should be searched, and inquiries made. If the individual kept a safe deposit box, it is possible the will is located in the box. If the safe deposit box is jointly owned, the co-owner should be able to search its contents. However, if the safe deposit box was solely owned by the decedent, a court order may be necessary to gain access to the contents. The bank representative will be able to supply the personal representative with the necessary requirements.

The individuals who would likely have knowledge concerning a will would be relatives, friends or personal advisors, such as the decedent's lawyer or accountant. Such individuals may know whether a will was ever executed, and where it may be located.

Proving the Will

Once the will has been located, it must be submitted to the proper court for validation. It must be established that the will was executed by the decedent in conformity with the laws of the particular state in which the decedent had his or her legal residence.

There are certain requirements that must be followed in order to make a valid will, which may vary from state to state. Generally, in order to make a valid will, the decedent must have been of the required legal age and mentally fit when the will was executed. Each state has a minimum age requirement for making a will. The majority of states, as well as the Uniform Probate Code, designate age 18 as the minimum age for making a will.

There are also technical requirements for the drafting of a valid will, according to the applicable state law. Generally, the will must be typewritten, signed before two or three witnesses, and dated. The will must also include the appointment of the personal representative.

If there have been minor changes to a will, a separate document—known as a codicil—may have been drafted to make additions or deletions. In order to be valid, any codicils must have been executed in the same manner as the will. A sample codicil is set forth in the Appendix.

In general, wills do not have to be notarized, but in some states, the witnesses can sign and have notarized a "self-proving affidavit," which eliminates the need for a witness to testify at the probate proceedings. A sample self-proving affidavit is set forth in the Appendix.

If the will is not self-proving, the witnesses who signed the will must attest to its validity and the decedent's signature. Affidavits must be signed by the witnesses and notarized. Once the sworn affidavits are returned, they should be filed with the court along with the will and any necessary forms for opening the estate.

A sample witness deposition is set forth in the Appendix.

Some courts require a hearing at which time the witnesses may be required to testify. If the will is not self-proving and the witnesses cannot be located, the testimony of other witnesses as to the authenticity of the signatures of the witnesses and decedent may be required.

Disinheritance

With few exceptions, an individual is not required to leave any property to any person unless they wish to do so. Thus, if a person is not named in the decedent's will, they will have no claim to the decedent's property after he or she dies. For example, an individual is permitted to disinherit a child. However, the decedent's intention to do so must be clearly stated in the will to avoid a claim against the estate by that child. In general, to disinherit a child, the will must expressly state the decedent's intention to do so either by including such a clause in the will, or by leaving the disinherited child a very small gift, such as one dollar, which for all practical purposes would constitute a disinheritance.

Disinheriting a spouse is more complicated. In the majority of states, one simply cannot disinherit a spouse unless the spouse waives his or her right to a portion of the estate. In the absence of such a waiver, the spouse is generally entitled to at least one-third of the decedent's estate.

Most states permit the surviving spouse to choose between the will provisions or receiving a certain portion of the estate according to the state's law. This is known as the spouse's right of election. The purpose of this law is to prevent a disinheritance of the spouse which might cause the disinherited spouse to become destitute. The portion of the estate available to a surviving spouse varies greatly from state to state, thus the reader is advised to check the law of his or her jurisdiction.

Contesting the Will

In certain instances, a will may be contested. A will may be contested on either procedural or substantive grounds.

Procedurally, if a will does not meet all of the legal requirements of the applicable state's statutes, it must be declared void.

The most common substantive ground for a successful will contest is proof of the testator's lack of mental capacity at the time he or she executed the will. In addition, if it can be shown that a will, or any of its parts, was executed under undue influence—*i.e.*, by coercion or force—the will, or that part of it executed under undue influence, is void.

A person who wants to contest a will must file his or her objections to the will with the court within a certain time period after the personal representative has notified interested parties of probate. A formal hearing must be held by the court to determine the issues raised by the will contestant. The personal representative is responsible for defending the will's validity.

A successful will contestant generally receives that share of the estate he or she would have received under state intestacy laws. If the will contest concerns the validity of two or more existing wills, the successful will contestant will receive his or her share according to the will which is proven valid. In addition, a successful will contestant's legal fees are generally paid from the estate's assets. Thus, prolonged will contest litigation can seriously deplete the assets of the estate.

CHAPTER 3:

INTESTACY

In General

To die without having made a valid will is to die *intestate*, a fairly common occurrence. Some people never consider making a will because they believe they have many years of life ahead of them or because they believe they have not accumulated enough assets to justify making a will. Others just never get around to making a will.

In some situations, the deceased may have executed a will, but later rendered it wholly or partially invalid by altering it. Any alterations made to a will after it is executed are prohibited without the attendant formalities. Further, if a will is successfully contested, the decedent will be deemed to have died intestate.

Procedure

Intestacy procedures are determined according to the state in which the decedent maintained his or her legal residence. To begin the proceeding, the appropriate forms must be filed with the court in place of the will. The court will then hold a hearing to appoint a personal representative to administer the decedent's estate. Some states permit the family members to elect the personal representative.

When it is determined that a person has died intestate, his or her estate must be distributed according to the state's statutes concerning intestate succession—the law of descent and distribution. Depending on the state, administration of the decedent's estate may require court supervision.

Although state statutes are not uniform concerning the manner of distribution, most state intestacy laws provide that the estate passes in varying percentages to the decedent's spouse and children. If the decedent was not married and had no children, the estate usually passes to the decedent's siblings and/or parents.

A table outlining the various state rules of inheritance is set forth in the Appendix.

Nevertheless, if the heirs can agree to a different division of the decedent's assets, the state distribution requirements may be waived.

When there are minor children involved, the court must appoint a guardian to care for the children and manage their inheritance until they reach the age of majority. The child's share of the estate is held in trust by the court-appointed guardian until that time. If there is a surviving parent, he or she is usually appointed as the guardian of the children's person and property.

CHAPTER 4:

THE PERSONAL REPRESENTATIVE

In General

The term "personal representative" has been adopted by the Uniform Probate Code to refer to the individual responsible for administering a decedent's estate, whether or not the decedent died intestate. The personal representative may be named in the will or, in the case of intestacy, appointed by the court or elected by the heirs.

Many state statutes have also adopted the term "personal representative" to replace the traditional use of the masculine and feminine terms—executor or executrix—to refer to the administrator named in a will, as well as the masculine and feminine terms—administrator or administratrix—to refer to the administrator of an intestate's estate.

The personal representative is usually a family member or friend of the decedent. If the decedent was married, the surviving spouse is usually appointed as the personal representative.

Responsibilities of the Personal Representative

As discussed below, and depending on the size of the decedent's estate, the tasks the personal representative may have to perform in opening the decedent's estate for probate, and completing the probate process, can be numerous.

For example, the personal representative is responsible for locating the will and the witnesses, and submitting the will and the appropriate witness affidavits and forms to the probate court.

The personal representative is also responsible for locating and preparing an inventory of all of the decedent's assets. The personal representative must also distribute those assets according to the decedent's wishes, or the state's intestacy laws if the decedent died without a will.

If the decedent's estate has any existing claims against any third parties—*e.g.*, a claim for wrongful death resulting from an automobile accident involving a negligent driver—the personal representative is responsible for seeing that the claim is pursued. The personal representative is responsible for hiring an attorney to represent the decedent's claim and for collecting any monies which would be due the decedent's estate as a result of a settlement or judgment.

Conversely, the personal representative is also responsible for seeing that any claims that are made against the decedent's estate, or taxes that are owed, are satisfied in a manner most advantageous to the estate.

Opening the Estate

It is the responsibility of the personal representative to make a formal application to the court for appointment, even when he or she has been named in the decedent's will. This form is generally submitted with the will and any other necessary documents to the court in order to "open the estate." The form is commonly referred to as a probate petition.

A sample probate petition is set forth in the Appendix.

The law may require the personal representative to post a bond. This is accomplished by paying a small fee to protect the assets of the estate from negligent or intentional mishandling by the personal representative. The cost of posting a bond is generally deducted from the estate. A will may waive this requirement.

Notification

The personal representative is responsible for notifying all interested persons about the individual's death. Such notification is generally required to be personally served or served by mail. Interested persons include but are not limited to beneficiaries, heirs and creditors. This notice must include the fact that the personal representative has applied to the court for formal appointment, and has opened the estate for probate. The reader is advised to check the law of his or her jurisdiction concerning the manner in which notice must be made.

A sample Notice of Probate is set forth in the Appendix.

Proper notice may also require publication in an approved newspaper circulating in the area where the decedent legally resided. Such notice serves to inform both creditors and interested persons of the opening of the estate.

Once the required notices are made, and the requisite proof of notice is filed with the court, the personal representative's application for appointment is generally approved. The personal representative is then given letters of administration—also referred to as letters testamentary—which serve as official proof that the personal representative is authorized to administer the decedent's estate.

A sample court order issuing letters testamentary is set forth in the Appendix.

Estate Accounts

The personal representative is responsible for opening a bank account in the name of the estate. All income from the estate should be deposited in this account, and all costs of estate administration should be paid from this account. Estate assets should always be kept separate from the personal funds of the personal representative. It is important that the personal representative maintain accurate financial records during administration of the estate. This will be helpful in preparing a final accounting of the estate for the court.

CHAPTER 5:

ADMINISTERING THE ESTATE

In General

Under present law, probating a will is a largely administrative procedure. Depending on the size of the estate to be administered and the applicable state law, the personal representative generally selects a probate procedure. The three most common procedures are supervised, unsupervised and small estate administration. These three procedures are discussed in more detail below.

Supervised Administration

Supervised administration is the usual manner in which an estate is administered. The reader is advised to check the law of his or her jurisdiction concerning the availability of unsupervised administration. However, even in those states which permit both supervised and unsupervised estate administration, the court may require supervised administration if it determines that the personal representative is not qualified to act unsupervised.

Supervised administration merely dictates that, at certain stages of administration, the personal representative file the required forms with the court for approval. For example, the personal representative may be required to obtain court approval before distributing assets or paying claims. The personal representative may also be required, on occasion, to make court appearances.

Unsupervised Administration

Unsupervised administration is available in states which have adopted the Uniform Probate Code, and other states which have made specific provisions for it under certain circumstances. Unsupervised administration generally requires the consent of all interested parties, and an interested person may request the court to supervise either all or part of the administration of the estate.

Unsupervised administration is less formal and has few reporting requirements. In fact, once letters of administration have been issued to the personal representative by the court, the estate can be settled without further court intervention.

The personal representative is responsible for preparing an inventory of the decedent's estate, paying all valid claims, and distributing the remaining assets. The personal representative need not report to the court, but is accountable to the heirs. Some courts may require a final accounting to be filed.

Small Estate Administration

Small estate administration refers to a simplified procedure for probating a small qualifying estate. In general, an estate qualifies for small estate administration in most states if (i) there is no solely owned real property; and (ii) the value of the estate does not exceed the state mandated maximum.

The monetary ceiling is based on the value of probate assets solely owned by the decedent. Jointly owned assets, insurance proceeds and other death benefits are generally excluded when valuing the estate to determine if it qualifies for small estate administration. Depending on the state, a number of additional exclusions may apply. Thus, an estate which at first appears too large for small estate administration may qualify once all of the exclusions are deducted from the value of the gross estate. The reader is advised to check the law of his or her own jurisdiction to determine the applicable exclusions.

If an estate qualifies for small estate administration, probate generally involves following several basic steps. The person handling administration of the estate is referred to as a claimant instead of a personal representative. In some states, the claimant must be a family member, such as the surviving spouse.

In general, there are two types of small estate administration: (i) summary administration; and (ii) administration unnecessary.

Summary administration is a shortened probate process which generally requires the claimant to provide notice of administration to all interested persons. In addition, an inventory of the estate assets is usually required to be filed with the court. Administration unnecessary does not, as the name implies, require any probate administration.

Small estate administration is generally accomplished by means of a (i) court order, or (ii) by affidavit.

Administration by Court Order

In states which require administration by court order, an inventory and appraisal of the estate's assets, and any other necessary documentation, must be filed with the court along with the petition for small estate administration.

If the petition is granted, the court will issue an order authorizing transfer of title, or the release of estate assets, to the claimant. The claimant presents the order to persons who are holding estate assets to obtain their release, or to whoever is responsible for transferring title to estate assets.

Administration by Affidavit

Most states simply require a claimant to complete an affidavit and file it with the court. The affidavit must be signed by the claimant and notarized. As with the court order, an original notarized affidavit is presented to persons who are holding estate assets to obtain their release, or to whoever is responsible for transferring title to estate assets.

Ancillary Administration

If a decedent owned property outside of his or her state of legal residence, a separate probate proceeding must be initiated. This is known as ancillary administration. Depending on the law of the state where the property is located, a personal representative may have to be named in that state to administer the assets located there.

CHAPTER 6:

INVENTORY

In General

The personal representative is responsible for assessing the value of the estate. A preliminary estimate of the value of the decedent's estate may be required when the estate is opened. A preliminary estimate assists the personal representative in budgeting for the expenses of operating the estate during the administration process.

Further, depending on the preliminary valuation, the estate may qualify for small estate administration, a very simple process preferable to both supervised and unsupervised administration. Small estate administration is further discussed in Chapter 5.

Locating Assets of the Estate

Within a certain time period following the opening of the estate, the personal representative must complete a more formal inventory and appraisal of the estate. A search for all of the decedent's assets and debts must be undertaken in order to properly inventory the estate. Depending on the state, the inventory may include both probate and nonprobate assets.

Probate assets generally consist of all of the decedent's real and personal property, including but not limited to homes, motor vehicles, bank accounts, household items, jewelry and personal effects. The personal representative should, on behalf of the estate, take possession of all probate assets of the estate. The letters of administration give the personal representative the authority to take possession of such assets and third parties are obligated to promptly transfer title or turn over the assets to the personal representative.

Nonprobate assets would include any jointly owned property, and property which names an individual beneficiary, such as life insurance proceeds, pension and certain trusts. Nonprobate assets pass directly to the named beneficiary or co-owner. However, jointly owned property that does not provide for a right of survivorship is generally deemed a probate asset to the extent of the portion owned by the decedent.

If the personal representative is unfamiliar with the decedent's affairs, information concerning assets and debts may be ascertained by contacting the decedent's relatives, friends, employment and business associates, and banking institutions. All of the decedent's files should be searched for receipts, bills, loan papers, warranties or other evidence of assets and debts.

The decedent may have left with his or her will, detailed instructions and information to assist the personal representative in carrying out his or her wishes. This information is often provided in the form of a letter attached to the will.

Useful information would include:

1. The location of the original and any copies of the decedent's will.

2. The names and addresses of the persons the decedent designated as guardians of his or her minor children, if applicable.

3. The account numbers for all decedent's savings, checking and other bank accounts; the decedent's safe deposit box number and the location of the safe deposit box key; and the location and address of the decedent's banks and the name of the bank officer at each of the banks.

4. The account numbers for all of the decedent's credit card accounts.

5. The decedent's burial instructions and cemetery lot information.

6. Information concerning the decedent's life insurance policies and the location of the policies.

7. Information concerning any other insurance the decedent may have which could be used to indemnify the estate against any claims which may be brought against it, such as malpractice, homeowners and automobile insurance.

8. The location and description of personal property which may be in the possession of someone else, such as artwork on loan to a museum.

9. A schedule of personal loans of money or property which the decedent may have made, and which are yet outstanding.

10. The names and addresses of persons who may have information concerning the decedent's financial affairs, such as his or her attorney, accountant, stockbroker, etc.

11. Information concerning past employment and pension, retirement or profit-sharing plan entitlements.

12. Personal documents, such as the decedent's birth certificate, social security card, marriage certificate, divorce papers (if applicable), passport, etc.

This information assists the personal representative in administering the decedent's will.

Complete and accurate tax records enable the personal representative to better handle any claims made against the estate by the taxing authorities that might otherwise be inexplicable. Records and books concerning any loans the decedent may have made, or debts he or she may have incurred, better enable the personal representative to collect on monies payable to the estate and/or avoid paying out fraudulent claims against the estate.

Appraising the Assets

The personal representative is responsible for having each item appraised so that the value of the estate can be determined. Appraisal of general items may be undertaken by the personal representative with the assistance of certain valuation guides, such as the "blue book" for automobile valuation.

More unique items, such as jewelry or family heirlooms, may be appraised by a professional knowledgeable in the particular area. Real estate may be appraised by a real estate appraiser. The costs of professional appraisers may be paid out of the estate account.

Final Inventory and Appraisal

A copy of the final inventory and appraisal should be filed with the court, and copies should be sent to all interested parties.

CHAPTER 7:

DEBTS

In General

Most people die leaving behind a number of unpaid bills. Of course, medical and funeral bills often follow a death. There may be outstanding household bills and credit card debts. The personal representative generally collects all of the bills mailed to the decedent's home. Settling these debts is a part of estate administration. As discussed in Chapter 4, the publication of a notice in an approved newspaper also serves to inform the decedent's creditors of the opening of the estate.

Payment of Claims

Creditors are required to present their claims within a certain time period, after which all claims are barred. Most states require that creditors' claims be submitted to the court, however, some states allow the personal representative to accept the claims directly.

The personal representative is responsible for accumulating all of the claims, evaluating them and paying all valid claims. If the personal representative is not satisfied that a particular claim is valid, he or she will mail a notice of disallowance to the particular creditor. The notice may disallow all or part of the creditor's claim. The creditor must then respond within a certain time period after receiving the disallowance.

After the time period for submitting claims has expired, the personal representative will pay all valid claims, including taxes. Payment of large claims may require court approval. If the estate does not have enough assets to pay all of the claims, certain preferred claims must be paid before the rest of the assets are distributed. Preferred claims may include probate fees and funeral expenses. If the estate lacks liquid assets, the distributees may contribute cash into the estate account rather than suffer the forced sale of an asset.

Real Property

Most estates include real property, the sale of which may be necessary to raise money for estate expenses or distribution. This entails all of the tasks normally associated with the sale of real property, including hiring professionals such as real estate brokers, appraisers and lawyers. Further, one must be familiar with the particular state's homestead exemption law which may prevent any sale while the property is occupied by a surviving spouse or children.

CHAPTER 8:

TRANSFERRING PROPERTY

In General

Most estates have assets which can be transferred directly to the beneficiaries—such as the heirs or the surviving spouse—or to one or more co-owners, without going through the probate process. Thus, transfer of these properties can be accomplished before the probate estate is closed. As discussed in Chapter 6, the personal representative must first classify the decedent's assets—both real and personal property—to distinguish between probate and nonprobate assets.

Jointly Owned Property

It must be determined whether assets which were co-owned by the decedent and one or more other individuals pass to the surviving co-owners. Some states deem all property owned by a married couple as containing a right of survivorship. Other states require the title to certain property to specifically state that there is a right of survivorship. The reader is advised to check the law of his or her own jurisdiction concerning specific requirements in this regard.

A right of survivorship generally means that the surviving owners of a certain piece of property automatically take title to the portion owned by the decedent upon his or her death. This form of ownership is generally referred to as *joint tenancy*. Some states require that the title specifically state that there is a right of survivorship.

Unless otherwise provided for in the ownership papers, each of the surviving co-owners would receive an equal share of the decedent's interest in the property. If there is only one surviving co-owner, he or she would become the owner of the whole property.

As it pertains to married couples, joint tenancy is generally referred to as "tenancy by the entirety." This infers that each of the spouses owns the entirety of the property, and that upon the death of one spouse, the surviving spouse continues as owner of the whole property.

In order to accomplish the transfer of jointly owned property, the state may require documentation including but not limited to proof of the death of the decedent, such as a certified copy of the death certificate; and proof that the property was jointly owned and that the surviving co-owners have the right to the decedent's share of the property. The reader is advised to check the law of his or her own jurisdiction to determine the necessary forms which must be filed to effectuate the transfer.

Community Property States

There are eight community property states including Arizona, California, Idaho, Louisiana, Nevada, New Mexico, Texas and Washington. In community property states, all property and earnings acquired during the marriage, excluding gifts or inheritances, are deemed community property.

Community property does not include a right of survivorship, thus the surviving spouse does not automatically take ownership over the decedent's one-half share of the property. The decedent's share of the property is generally subject to the probate process, and must pass by will to the designated beneficiary, or according to the state's intestacy laws. Some community property states have special provisions eliminating the necessity for probate when the property will pass to the surviving spouse.

Life Insurance and Pension Plan Proceeds

The proceeds from a life insurance policy, or pension plan, are not subject to probate, provided that the named beneficiary is not the decedent's estate. After the completion of certain required forms, the proceeds are paid directly to the named beneficiaries. If the named beneficiary is the decedent's estate, then the policy is subject to probate.

It is important to determine whether there are any additional sources of death benefits to which the decedent's heirs may be entitled, including social security benefits; veterans benefits; employee benefits, such as profit-sharing plans; union benefits; or benefits derived from other private retirement plans.

CHAPTER 9:

TAXATION

In General

An important aspect of probating an estate concerns the filing of tax returns and payment of any taxes owed. The tax returns are filed with the state or federal taxing authorities during estate administration. The taxes are paid out of the estate's assets.

Types of Tax Returns

There are a number of tax returns which may have to be filed during administration of the decedent's estate. These may include the decedent's personal federal, state and/or local income tax returns; the estate federal and/or state income tax returns; the state inheritance or estate tax return; and the federal estate tax return.

A small estate may incur little or no tax consequences, thus, the returns will generally be simpler to complete than a larger estate. If the tax situation is particularly complex, the personal representative may require the assistance of a professional accountant in completing and filing the returns.

Income Tax

Decedent's Personal Income Tax

A decedent's income earned during the tax year in which he or she dies is subject to income tax to the extent the income exceeds the allowable deductions and exemptions. The personal representative is required to file a federal income tax return and pay any taxes owed. A state income tax return may have to be filed as well.

Estate Income Tax

An estate may generate income from a number of sources during the period of administration, such as rental or interest income. The personal representative is required to file federal and estate income tax returns on behalf of the decedent's estate to the extent the estate's income exceeds the appropriate exemptions for the tax year.

Estate Tax

The Federal Estate Tax

Federal estate tax, also known as death tax, is the tax imposed on the right to transfer property by death. Thus, the responsible party for paying estate tax is the decedent's estate, not the inheritors of the property. All property owned by the deceased may be subject to payment of federal estate taxes, whether or not the transfer avoids probate, including life insurance.

If the value of the decedent's *gross estate* is over $600,000, an estate tax return must be filed. However, since the filing requirement is based on the gross estate, and does not take into account items such as the allowable exemptions, taxes will not necessarily be due. To determine whether the estate will incur federal estate tax, one should first estimate the net worth of the property of the estate. Allowable exemptions may then be deducted, including: (1) the marital deduction, which provides an exemption for all property left to the surviving spouse; (2) the charitable organization exemption, which provides an exemption for all gifts made to a tax-exempt charity; and (3) the $600,000 threshold exemption. Keep in mind, however, that any taxable gifts made during the decedent's lifetime can reduce the $600,000 exemption accordingly.

State Inheritance and Estate Tax

States are also empowered to impose death taxes on their residents. Generally, such taxes are assessed on the resident's personal property and any real property located in the state. The reader is advised to check the law of his or her own jurisdiction to determine whether their state imposes death taxes, and in which situations such taxes are assessed.

Some states assess death taxes only on estates that are subject to federal estate tax, as discussed above. Other states impose an *inheritance tax*, which is a tax on the inheritor's right to receive property from the estate.

If the decedent maintained residences in more than one state, his or her *domicile* must be determined. The decedent's domicile is the state with which the decedent had the most significant ties, such as the state in which he or she voted, carried on his or her business, and owned his or her primary residence. Of course, it would be to the estate's benefit if the decedent's domicile is determined to be in the state that imposes little or no death taxes. Presently, every state except Nevada has some type of death tax.

A sample New York State Succession Tax Return is set forth in the Appendix.

CHAPTER 10:

FEES

In General

The personal representative of the decedent's estate is entitled to compensation for his or her services in administering the probate estate. In addition, if there was an estate lawyer involved, he or she would also be entitled to compensation for his or her services to the estate.

The Personal Representative

Most family members and close friends who agree to act as personal representatives for the estate do not collect a fee for their services. If they do collect a fee, it is usually a nominal amount. If an attorney is named in the decedent's will to act as personal representative, or is retained by the family or appointed by the court to administer the estate, there will likely be fees incurred.

Fees would also be payable by the estate if a bank or other corporation is named to serve as personal representative. This is often the case when the estate is large and complex, and there are no family members or friends available or capable of handling administration. Unfortunately, this usually results in higher fees because corporations often hire lawyers to assist in the technical aspects of administration.

The Estate Lawyer

An estate lawyer may be hired by the personal representative to assist in administering the estate, particularly when there are complex issues which need to be resolved. Some personal representatives hire a lawyer to oversee the entire probate process. The result is that the lawyer may charge a considerable fee—usually computed as a percentage of the estate—for performing duties which can easily be performed by the personal representative. As discussed below, it is more cost effective to the estate for the personal representative to undertake most of the probate work, and to retain a lawyer on an hourly basis for specific purposes as the need arises.

Fee Limitations and Arrangements

In order to protect the estate from being depleted by excessive fees, laws exist which place a cap on the fees that can be charged for services performed. Nevertheless, the state's legally permissible fees, usually based on a percentage of the estate, can still be quite a drain on the assets of the estate.

In many cases, the fees charged do not adequately reflect the services which were performed. If a lawyer is hired to assist in probate, it is important that a written fee agreement be obtained prior to his or her rendering any services.

One must understand the manner in which fees for services rendered will be calculated so that a professional may be hired whose rates will be most cost effective. In general, fees are charged either on an hourly rate, or as a percentage of the estate.

An hourly rate may be the most advantageous fee structure because it reflects payment for actual work performed. Conversely, if the fee is based on a percentage of the estate, it will quite likely be disproportionate to the amount of work performed on behalf of the estate. It is customary in many states for probate fees to be computed on a percentage basis regardless of services performed, although many states are attempting to enforce a "reasonable fee" standard, particularly as it pertains to estate lawyers.

Fee Reduction

An interested person may file a petition with the court for a reduction in the fees charged by a personal representative or estate lawyer. However, it is often difficult to prove that the fee is unreasonable without documentation of the time and effort expended. If administration required mostly clerical work and the filing of forms, the petitioner may be able to show that, on an hourly basis, the requested fee is clearly disproportionate to the work performed.

The personal representative or estate lawyer must then demonstrate to the court how his or her fee is reasonable and customary. The court will review all of the evidence and testimony and render a decision. In the meantime, the closing of the estate and distribution of assets will be suspended while the fee reduction petition is pending.

CHAPTER 11:

CLOSING THE ESTATE

In General

The personal representative is responsible for filing the forms necessary to close the estate and release him or her from any further responsibility. In order to close the estate, a final accounting may be required. In some states, the personal representative is not released from responsibility until all of the assets are distributed, and a final report is filed with the court.

The Final Accounting

The final accounting details the assets and expenses of the estate, including taxes, and the balance of the estate to be distributed. If administration of the estate is court supervised, the accounting must be filed with the court. If administration is unsupervised, the personal representative gives the final accounting to the heirs.

Assets

The final accounting must detail all assets of the estate, including those assets uncovered in the initial inventory of the estate, and any assets recovered during estate administration.

Expenses

The final accounting must detail all estate expenses, including all of the decedent's bills and outstanding obligations at the time of death; burial expenses; fees for the personal representative and other professionals hired by the estate during administration; and any ongoing estate expenses.

Taxes

After deducting the expenses from the assets, the applicable taxes must be calculated on the estate balance less any exemptions.

Balance of Estate

After payment of the taxes, the balance of the estate is distributed to the decedent's beneficiaries and/or heirs. The final accounting should include the intended distribution, with a detailed list of the assets to be distributed and the recipients.

The Supervised Estate

Court supervised estate administration requires that the final accounting be filed with the court. The accounting should include copies of all applicable receipts and proof of payment, such as canceled checks. An audit may be conducted to confirm the accuracy of the accounting figures. Following the audit, the estate may be formally closed. Generally, this may be accomplished either by petition to the court, or by sworn statement.

Court Petition

If closing is sought by court petition, the personal representative must submit the final accounting to the court with the petition. After the court has reviewed the petition, it sets a hearing date. Notice of the hearing date must be sent to all interested persons, including any creditors of the estate. At the final hearing, the court may resolve any outstanding issues, such as a fee reduction request. After all issues have been resolved, the court approves the final accounting and proposed distribution of the estate, and orders that distribution proceed.

Sworn Statement

If closing is sought by sworn statement, the personal representative must submit a form to the court which details, under oath, all of the steps which were taken in administering the estate. Copies of the final accounting and sworn statement must be distributed to all interested persons.

CHAPTER 12:

ASSET DISTRIBUTION

In General

The remainder of the property left in the estate after payment of claims, expenses and taxes, is distributed according to the decedent's will, or according to the state intestacy laws, if there is no valid will. Some debts, such as liens on certain assets, like real estate or automobiles, are not paid from the estate, but are assumed by the inheritor of the particular asset.

Beneficiaries

The beneficiaries named in the decedent's will are those persons, or entities the decedent wishes to receive his or her assets upon death. A beneficiary may be a (i) primary; (ii) alternate; or (iii) residuary beneficiary.

The *primary beneficiary* is the decedent's first choice to receive a specified gift of property. An *alternate beneficiary* may be named to receive that specific property if the primary beneficiary predeceases the decedent, and the will was not amended to change the primary beneficiary.

The *residuary beneficiary* is the person or entity which receives the balance of the decedent's estate—the *residuary estate*—if any, after all of the specific gifts of property are made. If alternate beneficiaries are not named for any specific gift of property, and the primary beneficiary predeceases the decedent, that property also passes to the residuary beneficiary.

Survivorship Periods

The will generally provides for a survivorship period—a specified period of time during which the beneficiary must survive the decedent in order to inherit under the will. If the primary beneficiary dies shortly after the decedent, and there is no established survivorship period, the property intended for the primary beneficiary will pass under the primary beneficiary's will, in which case it may end up in the hands of strangers to the decedent. If the will provides for a survivorship period, and the decedent's primary beneficiary dies within that time period, e.g. 60 days, the property will pass instead to the alternate or residuary beneficiary under the original decedent's will.

Distribution In Kind

If there is not enough cash in the estate to fulfill specific bequests left by the will, the personal representative may have to sell estate assets. However, if a forced sale of the assets is not cost effective, most states provide for *distribution in kind.*

Distribution in kind refers to the surrender of certain assets of the estate in place of cash value. For the purposes of distribution in kind, the asset is valued as of the date of distribution instead of the date of death. Nevertheless, if the heirs demand cash, the physical assets of the estate may have to be sold.

Further, if a residuary beneficiary requests that a specific asset remain in the estate, or if the current market value of the specific asset does not equal the cash bequest, distribution in kind is not permissible and the asset cannot be distributed in lieu of the cash bequest.

Intestate Distribution

If the decedent did not leave a valid will, the estate assets must be distributed according to the state's laws of intestacy. The personal representative simply follows the provisions of the state's intestacy laws in distributing the property to the heirs.

A table of state rules of inheritance is set forth in the Appendix.

Minors

If the decedent leaves property to a minor child, any substantial gift must be supervised by an adult guardian who must be named in the will. In most cases, the decedent simply names his or her surviving spouse. If there is no surviving spouse, the person who has been designated as the personal guardian to take custody of the child may also act as the guardian for the child's property.

This adult guardian is obligated to use the money to provide for the needs of the child, and is required to regularly report to the court on how the money is being spent. In addition, the guardian generally needs permission from the court before investing the child's property. When the child reaches the age of majority, the guardianship relationship automatically ends and the child is entitled to receive the remainder of his or her property.

Property can also be left to minor children by means of a trust, as further discussed in Chapter 14.

Appointing a Guardian for Minor Children

If the decedent had minor children when he or she died, the children are usually placed in, or remain in, the custody of their surviving parent. If both parents die simultaneously or if the one parent available to care for the children dies, the children must be placed in the custody of another responsible adult—a personal guardian.

The will usually names the person the decedent wishes to fulfill the role of guardian of his or her minor children. Although the decedent is free to name whoever he or she desires, the decedent's choice usually requires court approval unless, of course, it is the surviving parent. In most cases, the court will abide by the decedent's wishes, unless there is a question of the designated person's fitness or someone contests the designation. The will may also name an alternate person to act as guardian, in the event his or her first choice is unavailable, unwilling, or unable to serve at the time of the decedent's death.

CHAPTER 13:

THE UNIFORM PROBATE CODE

In General

The Uniform Probate Code (UPC) was drafted by the National Conference of Commissioners on Uniform State Laws and approved in 1969 by the American Bar Association in response to a public outcry for probate reform. The UPC's purpose is to simplify and make uniform the law of wills and estates among the states, and to promote the speedy, efficient and cost-effective administration of estates.

The majority of the states have not yet enacted the UPC in its entirety, although many states have adopted portions of the law or have enacted their own legislation patterned after UPC provisions.

It would be impossible to reproduce the entire Uniform Probate Code in this legal almanac. However, for the reader's reference, the Table of Contents of the Uniform Probate Code is set forth in the Appendix as a useful guide in locating specific sections of law within the UPC. An overview of the UPC's major provisions is set forth below.

Overview of the Uniform Probate Code

The UPC contains eight articles with numerous sub-parts, as follows:

Article I - General Provisions

Article I of the UPC is broken down into four sub-parts, and contains general information concerning the UPC, including the purpose of the UPC and rules of construction; general definitions of the terms used throughout; jurisdictional matters; and notice requirements.

Article II - Intestate Succession and Wills

Article II is the second largest article of the UPC. It contains nine sub-parts. Article II contains the substantive law concerning the execution of wills and intestate distribution.

Article III - Probate of Wills and Administration

Article III is the largest article of the UPC. It contains twelve sub-parts detailing probate procedures and administration of decedent's estates. Article III presents the UPC's version of the procedures discussed in this legal almanac.

Article IV - Foreign Personal Representatives -Ancillary Administration

Article IV of the UPC contains four sub-parts concerned with administration of the decedent's estate outside of his or her state of legal residence, and the appointment of a foreign personal representative to administer the ancillary estate.

Article V - Protection of Persons Under Disability and Their Property

Article V of the UPC contains five sub-parts concerned with the protection of persons who are disabled, e.g. by incapacity or minority, and the protection of their property, and provides for the appointment of guardians.

Article VI - Non-Probate Transfers

Article VI of the UPC contains two sub-parts concerned with the transfer of non-probate property during the administration of the decedent's estate.

Article VII - Trust Administration

Article VII of the UPC contains three sub-parts concerned with the administration of trusts, the duties and liabilities of the trustee, and the jurisdiction of the court in overseeing trust administration.

Article VIII - Effective Date and Repealer

Article VIII of the UPC provides for the effective date of the UPC and matters relating to amendment and repeal.

CHAPTER 14:

PROBATE AVOIDANCE

In General

Because the probate process can be time-consuming and expensive, there is growing support for probate reform. The probate process in England was drastically reformed in 1926, and is now a routine and efficient procedure, as it is in most countries.

In the United States, there are legal mechanisms for property to bypass a will, also known as probate avoidance methods. Such methods may include naming beneficiaries to receive life insurance proceeds, and pension and retirement plan distributions; joint ownership of property; setting up living trusts; and informal probate avoidance procedures.

Until reform is achieved in this country, many persons will continue to attempt to avoid it or to minimize the portions of their estates that are subject to the probate process.

Probate Exemptions

Some states provide various exemptions from the probate process by either allowing a certain amount of the deceased's property to be completely exempt from probate or subject to a much more simplified probate process than normal.

A table of state statutes concerning state law exceptions to conventional probate is set forth in the Appendix.

Jointly Owned Property

Any property held in joint tenancy by the decedent passes directly to the other joint tenants, each of whom is deemed to have an equal interest in the property. Married couples commonly hold deeds to marital real estate and bank accounts as joint tenants. However, some states have restricted or abolished joint tenancy.

Another form of real estate ownership, available only to married couples, is tenancy by the entirety. This type of arrangement also avoids probate, since each of the spouses is considered to hold title to the whole property and the death of one spouse does not affect the other spouse's ownership of the whole property. Similar to a joint tenancy, a tenancy by the entirety is grounded in the common-law theory that a husband and wife are one person.

Trusts

In General

A trust is the voluntary transfer of real or personal property, known as the trust corpus, trust assets, or trust principal, by a person—the *creator or settlor* of the trust—to a another party, known as the *trustee*.

The trustee is obligated to manage and invest the trust principal and to pay the trust income—and sometimes the trust principal, where trust income is insufficient—to or for the benefit of the beneficiaries of the trust, usually free of court intervention.

A trust may be used to provide financial security for the decedent's family, to avoid the time-consuming and expensive probate process after death, and in some cases, to minimize taxes. A trust can be particularly useful in providing for minor children, handicapped relatives, and loved ones who may have special needs.

There are many kinds of trusts. One which is created by will to take effect at the time of death is called a *testamentary trust*. If the trust is created during the decedent's lifetime, it is called an *inter vivos*, or living trust. A trust may be irrevocable or revocable, depending on the creator's retention of control over the trust. Some of the most common trusts are discussed below.

The Irrevocable Trust

An irrevocable trust is one that cannot be amended or revoked by its creator once it becomes effective. An irrevocable trust is a distinct legal entity from its creator, unlike the living trust, which is usually operated at the discretion of the creator until his or her death. Therefore, the trustee of the irrevocable trust must file income tax returns for the trust when it receives income above the statutory amount. The trustee's responsibilities also include distributing income or paying expenses, such as educational expenses, according to the terms of the trust.

An irrevocable trust can insulate the creator from estate and income taxation as long as he or she abandons all control over the trust. If the creator retains any control over the trust, he or she will not be shielded from such consequences of ownership.

The Revocable Living Trust

A revocable living trust is a legal entity set up and operated by the creator of the trust during his or her lifetime, for the benefit of those named in the trust. A revocable living trust is mainly used to avoid probate. It does not minimize estate taxes after death, nor does it change or lower the creator's income tax obligations during his or her life. The property placed in the trust can also be levied upon by the creator's creditors during his or her life.

The creator of a revocable living trust "places" property, either real or personal, into the trust by way of executing a legal document. The trust document names: (1) the trustee—the person who will manage the property—who is usually the creator of the trust; (2) the person who will carry out the terms of the trust when the creator dies, known as a *successor trustee*; and (3) the beneficiaries—the persons designated to receive the property after the creator dies.

The document also lists the property subject to the trust and, unlike an irrevocable trust, states that the creator can amend or revoke the trust at any time. This provision enables the creator to control the trust during his or her life, as desired. After the creator dies, however, the trust can no longer be amended or revoked. The person named as the successor trustee is obligated to transfer all property in the trust to the named beneficiaries.

Because the trust property does not pass by will, but goes directly to the named beneficiaries of the trust, there is no court involvement. After all of the property in the trust is transferred to the named beneficiaries, the trust ceases to exist.

Marital Living Trust

Since many married couples own property jointly, in addition to having separate living trusts set up for their own property, they can create a revocable marital living trust, in which they place their shared property. Each spouse designates beneficiaries for his or her respective share of the property.

Upon one spouse's death, the property is divided, and the deceased spouse's share of the property is transferred to his or her beneficiaries, which can include the surviving spouse. The surviving spouse's revocable living trust continues to exist until his or her death.

Childrens Trust

If one of the named beneficiaries in a trust is a minor at the time the creator dies, an adult guardian must manage the property for the minor's benefit until the age designated in the trust document. This differs from property left to a minor by will, in that the adult guardian is obligated to transfer bequeathed property to the minor beneficiary as soon as he or she reaches the legal age of majority—usually 18.

If there are concerns about the maturity and ability of beneficiaries to manage property at the age of 18, one should consider transferring property to these beneficiaries by way of a children's trust, which can be part of a living trust.

Upon death, if the child has reached the age designated in the trust, the trust property will be transferred directly to him or her. If the creator dies before the child reaches the designated age, however, the children's trust becomes irrevocable and is managed by the successor trustee of the decedent's living trust until the child reaches the designated age.

Spendthrift Trust

A spendthrift trust is usually set up on behalf of a beneficiary who the creator believes cannot properly manage money—i.e., the spendthrift. The beneficiary of a spendthrift trust receives the trust income from the trustee on a regular basis, but is unable to touch the trust principal. The creator can designate an age when the trust will end, at which time the trustee must transfer all of the property from the trust to the beneficiary.

Informal Probate Avoidance

Families often resort to what is known as informal probate avoidance, whereby the family bypasses the court and independently divides the deceased relative's property as his or her will—if there is one—directs. If there is no will, the family may divide the property according to the state's intestacy statutes or by mutual agreement.

Informal probate avoidance often occurs when the decedent's estate is very small, generally consisting entirely of personal property that is accessible to the family members. However, if the decedent has left any property that requires legal authority to transfer title, such as a house, formal probate procedures must be followed to obtain the legal authority to transfer title.

APPENDICES

APPENDIX 1:

SAMPLE WILL

I, Mary Jones, residing at 545 Main Street, in the Town of White Plains, Westchester County, in the State of New York, declare that this is my will. My Social Security Number is 555-55-5555.

FIRST: I revoke all wills and codicils that I have previously made.

SECOND: As used in this will, the term "specific bequest" refers to all specifically identified property that I give to one or more beneficiaries in this will. The term "residuary estate" refers to the rest of my property not otherwise specifically disposed of by this will or in any other manner. The term "residuary bequest" refers to my residuary estate that I give to one or more beneficiaries in this will.

THIRD: All personal property I give in this will through a specific or residuary bequest is given subject to any purchase-money security interest, and all real property I give in this will through a specific or residuary bequest is given subject to any deed of trust, mortgage, lien, assessment, or real property tax owed on the property. As used in this will, "purchase-money security interest" means any debt secured by collateral that was incurred for the purpose of purchasing that collateral. As used in this will, "non-purchase-money security interest" means any debt that is secured by collateral but which was not incurred for the purpose of purchasing that collateral.

FOURTH: Except for purchase money security interests on personal property passed in this will, and deeds of trust, mortgages, liens, taxes and assessments on real property passed in this will, I instruct my personal representative to pay all debts and expenses, including non-purchase-money secured debts on personal property, if any, owed by my estate as provided for by the laws of New York.

FIFTH: I instruct my personal representative to pay all estate and inheritance taxes, if any, assessed against property in my estate or against my beneficiaries as provided for by the laws of New York.

SIXTH: All the rest, residue and remainder of my estate, both real and personal, of whatsoever kind and nature and wheresoever possessed, or to which I in any way be entitled at the time of my decease, I give, devise and bequeath unto my beloved husband, JOHN JONES, if he survives me, absolutely.

SEVENTH: If my husband, JOHN JONES, shall have predeceased me, then I give, devise and bequeath my entire residuary estate, as aforesaid, unto my first alternate beneficiaries, my children, KATHLEEN JONES, born March 13, 1989; and JEANINE JONES, born November 15, 1981; and any other of my children who may be born after the date that this will is made, in equal shares. If any of my children shall have predeceased me, then I give, devise and bequeath my entire residuary estate, as aforesaid, unto my surviving children, in equal shares. I have not provided for my son, JAMES JONES, born March 27, 1973, in this will, because I have provided for him separately as a beneficiary of a life insurance policy. Notwithstanding the foregoing, if at the time of my decease, it is determined that I have no life insurance policy in effect which names my son, JAMES JONES, as beneficiary, then he is hereby named as an additional first alternate beneficiary under my will, to share equally with my other children named herein as first alternate beneficiaries.

EIGHTH: If my first alternate beneficiaries fail to survive me, I hereby give, devise and bequeath my entire residuary estate, as aforesaid, to my second alternate beneficiaries, in equal shares, as follows: To my father-in-law, CHRISTOPHER JONES, presently residing at 53 Dartmouth Street, Garden City, New York; to my father, ARTHUR SMITH, presently residing at 65-85 162nd Street, Flushing, New York; and to my mother, MARGARET SMITH, presently residing at 35-15 84th Street, Jackson Heights, New York. If any of the aforementioned second alternate beneficiaries shall have predeceased me, then I give, devise and bequeath my entire residuary estate, as aforesaid, unto the surviving second alternate beneficiaries, in equal shares.

NINTH: In the event that any of my children are minors at the time of my decease, I authorize my Personal Representative, as trustee, in his discretion, to retain the possession of the respective portion of such minors and accumulate the income therefrom during such minority, or pay over or apply the whole or any part of such principal and income to such minors, or for their support, maintenance, welfare and education, and the receipt of such payee shall be full acquittance to trustee. Any principal or income so retained or accumulated shall be paid to the minor upon attaining the age of twenty-one (21) years. Nothing herein contained shall be deemed to defer the vesting of any estate or interest in possession or otherwise.

TENTH: In the event that, upon my death, there is no living person who is entitled by law to the custody of my minor child or children, and who is available to assume such custody, I name my brother, MICHAEL SMITH, presently residing at 175 West 87th Street, Apt. 18-E, New York, New York 10024, as legal guardian of such child, to serve without bond.

ELEVENTH: When this will states that a beneficiary must survive me for the purpose of receiving a specific bequest or residuary bequest, he or she must survive me by 45 days. Notwithstanding the foregoing, property left to my spouse shall pass free of this 45-day survivorship requirement.

TWELFTH: Any specific bequest or residuary bequest made in this will to two or more beneficiaries shall be shared equally among them, unless unequal shares are specifically indicated.

THIRTEENTH: I name my husband, JOHN JONES, 545 Main Street, White Plains, New York, as my personal representative, to serve without bond. If this person shall for any reason fail to qualify or cease to act as personal representative, I name my brother, MICHAEL SMITH, 175 West 87th Street, Apt. 18-E, New York, New York 10024, as my personal representative, also to serve without bond.

FOURTEENTH: I direct my personal representative to take all actions legally permissible to have the probate of my will done as simply and as free of court supervision as possible under the laws of the state having jurisdiction over this will, including filing a petition in the appropriate court for the independent administration of my estate.

FIFTEENTH: I hereby grant to my personal representative the following powers, to be exercised as he or she deems to be in the best interests of my estate:

1. To retain property without liability for loss or depreciation resulting from such retention.

2. To dispose of property by public or private sale, or exchange, or otherwise, and receive and administer the proceeds as a part of my estate.

3. To vote stock, to exercise any option or privilege to convert bonds, notes, stocks or other securities belonging to my estate into other bonds, notes, stocks or other securities, and to exercise all other rights and privileges of a person owning similar property.

4. To lease any real property that may at any time form part of my estate.

5. To abandon, adjust, arbitrate, compromise, sue on or defend and otherwise deal with and settle claims in favor of or against my estate.

6. To continue or participate in any business which is a part of my estate, and to effect incorporation, dissolution or other change in the form of organization of the business.

7. To do all other acts which in his or her judgment may be necessary or appropriate for the proper and advantageous management, investment and distribution of my estate.

The foregoing powers, authority and discretion granted to my personal representative are intended to be in addition to the powers, authority and discretion vested in him or her by operation of law by virtue of his or her office, and may be exercised as often as is deemed necessary or advisable, without application to or approval by any court in any jurisdiction.

SIXTEENTH: If any beneficiary under this will in any manner, directly or indirectly, contests or attacks this will or any of its provisions, any share or interest in my estate given to the contesting beneficiary under this will is revoked and shall be disposed of in the same manner as if that contesting beneficiary had failed to survive me and left no living children.

SEVENTEENTH: If my spouse and I should die simultaneously, or under such circumstances as to render it difficult or impossible to determine who predeceased the other, I shall be conclusively presumed to have survived my spouse for purposes of this will.

I, Mary Jones, the testator, sign my name to this instrument, this 1st day of July, 1997. I hereby declare that I sign and execute this instrument as my last will, that I sign it willingly, and that I execute it as my free and voluntary act for the purposes therein expressed. I declare that I am of the age of majority and otherwise legally empowered to make a will, and under no constraint or undue influence. I hereby execute this will in the presence of ELEANOR JACKSON, EILEEN HARRISON and BARBARA CARTER, whom I have requested to act as witnesses.

_____
SIGNATURE LINE FOR TESTATRIX

In our presence, MARY JONES, the Testatrix, executed, published and declared that the foregoing instrument is her will, and in her presence and in the presence of each other we have signed our names below as witnesses this 1st day of July, 1997.

To the best of our knowledge, the testator is of the age of majority or otherwise legally empowered to make a will, is mentally competent, and under no constraint or undue influence.

We declare under penalty of perjury, that the foregoing is true and correct.

_____
SIGNATURE LINE FOR WITNESS #1
ADDRESS OF WITNESS #1

_____
SIGNATURE LINE FOR WITNESS #2
ADDRESS OF WITNESS #2

_____
SIGNATURE LINE FOR WITNESS #3
ADDRESS OF WITNESS #3

APPENDIX 2:

SAMPLE CODICIL TO A WILL

On July 1, 1997, I, MARY JONES, executed my will in the presence of the following witnesses:

1. Eleanor Jackson

2. Eileen Harrison

3. Barbara Carter

I hereby make this first codicil to my will, as follows:

Whereas in paragraph designated ELEVENTH of my will I appointed my husband, JOHN JONES, as my executor, I now wish to name my father, ARTHUR SMITH, to act as my executor, also to serve without bond.

I hereby execute this codicil on January 1, 19__, in the presence of Eleanor Jackson, Eileen Harrison and Barbara Carter, whom I requested to act as witnesses.

_____
Signature Line for Testatrix

In our presence, MARY JONES, the Testatrix, executed, published and declared that the foregoing instrument is the first codicil to his will, and in his presence and in the presence of each other we have signed our names below as witnesses this 1st day of January, 19__.

_____
Signature Line for Witness #1

_____
Signature Line for Witness #2

_____
Signature Line for Witness #3

APPENDIX 3:

SELF PROVING AFFIDAVIT

STATE OF [Name of State]

COUNTY OF [Name of County]

I, the undersigned, an officer authorized to administer oaths, certify that MARY JONES, the testatrix, and the witnesses, ELEANOR JACKSON, EILEEN HARRISON and BARBARA CARTER, whose names are signed to the attached instrument and whose signatures appear below, having appeared together before me and having first duly affirmed, each then declared to me that:

1. The attached or foregoing instrument is the last will of the testatrix;

2. The testatrix willingly and voluntarily declared, signed and executed the will in the presence of the witnesses;

3. The witnesses signed the will upon request by the testatrix, in the presence and hearing of the testatrix, and in the presence of each other;

4. To the best knowledge of each witness the testatrix was, at that time of the signing, of the age of majority and otherwise legally competent to make a will, of sound mind, and under no constraint or undue influence; and

5. Each witness was and is competent, and was then 18 years of age or older.

_____
Signature Line for Testatrix

_____
Signature Line for Witness #1
Address of Witness #1

_____
Signature Line for Witness #2
Address of Witness #2

_____
Signature Line for Witness #3
Address of Witness #3

Sworn to and acknowledged before me by the testatrix, MARY JONES, and by her witnesses, ELEANOR JACKSON, EILEEN HARRISON and BARBARA CARTER, this 1st day of January, 19__.

Notary Public Signature and Seal

APPENDIX 4:

SAMPLE DEPOSITION OF WITNESS

SURROGATE'S COURT: COUNTY OF BRONX
_____

Probate Proceeding,

Will of _____,

                          DEPOSITION
                          OF WITNESS

                Deceased.

_____

STATE OF NEW YORK	)
	ss.:
COUNTY OF BRONX	)

     I, _____, having been duly sworn, deposes and says:

     1.   I reside at _____.

     2.   I was acquainted with the decedent for ____ years, prior to his/her death on _____, 19___.

     3.   The subscription of the name of the said decedent to (a court-certified photographic reproduction of) the instrument now shown to me and about to be offered for probate as his/her Last Will and Testament, and bearing the date _____, 19___, was made by decedent at _____, in the State of New York, on _____, 19___, in the presence of myself and _____, the other subscribing witness(es).

     4.   At the time of making such subscription I knew that the said instrument so subscribed by him/her to be his/her Last Will and Testament, and I thereupon signed my name as a witness in his/her presence.

     5.   The said decedent at the time of so executing said instrument, was over eighteen years of age, and in my opinion of sound mind, memory and understanding, and not under any restraint or in any respect incompetent to make a will.

     6.   I also saw _____, the other subscribing witness(es) sign their name(s) as witness(es) at the end of said instrument, and know that he/she/they did so at the request and in the presence of said decedent.

     7.   Said decedent could read and write, as well as converse in the English language, and was neither deaf nor blind. The instrument was not executed by the decedent while be was confined in any hospital or sanitarium, nor while confined to his/her home or bed, because of any physical or mental condition, and said instrument was executed more than three months prior to the death of the decedent.*

*(If decedent could not read or write in the English language or was deaf or blind or confined to his or her home or hospitalized at the time of said execution, set forth such fact.)

8. Said instrument was not executed in multiplicate and is the only testamentary instrument executed on said occasion by said decedent.

9. Said instrument is now in the same condition as it was immediately following execution.

10. This affidavit was made at the request of _____.

11. The execution of said instrument now offered for probate was supervised by _____, an attorney at law of the State of New York.

12. So far as I know there can be no objection to the genuineness of said instrument or to the validity of its execution. I have no knowledge or information of any facts or circumstances which might raise any question as to the genuineness of said instrument or the validity of its execution.

_____
Signature of Witness

SWORN TO BEFORE ME THIS
____ DAY OF _____, 19____.

_____
NOTARY PUBLIC

APPENDIX 5: STATE RULES OF INHERITANCE

STATE	APPLICABLE STATUTE	BASIC INHERITANCE RULES
Alabama	Alabama Code, Title 43, §§43-1-1 et seq.	100% to surviving spouse if no surviving children or parents; $50,000 plus 1/2 of estate to surviving spouse if surviving children and all are issue of surviving spouse; 1/2 of estate to surviving spouse if surviving children and all not issue of surviving spouse; $100,000 plus 1/2 of estate to surviving spouse if surviving parents but no surviving children.
Alaska	Alaska Statutes, §13.11.005	100% to surviving spouse if no surviving children or parents; $50,000 plus 1/2 of estate to surviving spouse if surviving children and all issue of surviving spouse; 1/2 of estate to surviving spouse if surviving children and all not issue of surviving spouse; $50,000 plus 1/2 of estate to surviving spouse if surviving parents but no children.
Arizona	Arizona Revised Statutes, §§14-2101 et seq.	1/2 of all community property to surviving spouse; 100% of community property and separate property to surviving spouse if no surviving children or if surviving children and all are issue of surviving spouse; 1/2 of all community property and 1/2 of all separate property to surviving spouse if surviving children and all not issue of surviving spouse.
Arkansas	Arkansas Statutes Annotated, §§28-8-101 et seq.	Entire estate to surviving children or descendants of deceased children; if no such descendants then 100% to surviving spouse if married for 3 years; if not married for 3 years then 50% to surviving spouse and 50% to surviving parents; if no surviving children or spouse then 100% to surviving parents.
California	California Probate Code, §§1 et seq.	1/2 of all community property and 1/2 of all decedent's community property to surviving spouse; 100% of all separate property to surviving spouse if no surviving children, parents, siblings or issue of siblings; 1/2 of separate property to surviving spouse if one surviving child, issue of deceased child, surviving parent, or issue of parent; 1/3 of separate property if more than one surviving child or issue of two or more deceased children.
Colorado	Colorado Revised Statutes, §§15-1-101 et seq.,	100% to surviving spouse if no surviving children; $25,000 plus 1/2 of estate to surviving spouse if surviving children and all are issue of surviving spouse; 1/2 of estate to surviving spouse if surviving children and all not issue of surviving spouse.

PROBATE LAW

STATE	APPLICABLE STATUTE	BASIC INHERITANCE RULES
Connecticut	Connecticut General Statutes Annotated, §§45-1 et seq.	100% to surviving spouse if no surviving children, issue of deceased children, or surviving parents; $100,000 plus 1/2 of estate to surviving spouse if surviving children and all are issue of surviving spouse; 1/2 of estate to surviving spouse if surviving children and all not issue of surviving spouse; $100,000 plus 3/4 of estate to surviving spouse if surviving parents but no surviving children; if no surviving children or spouse, 100% to surviving parents.
Delaware	Delaware Code Annotated, Title 12, §§101 et seq.	100% to surviving spouse if no surviving children or parents; $50,000 plus 1/2 of personal estate and life estate in realty to surviving spouse if surviving children and all are issue of surviving spouse; 1/2 of personal estate and life estate in realty to surviving spouse if surviving children and all not issue of surviving spouse; $50,000 plus 1/2 of personal estate and life estate in realty to surviving spouse if surviving parent.
District of Columbia	District of Columbia Code, §§18-101 et seq.	100% to surviving spouse if no surviving children, parents, grandchildren, siblings or children of siblings; 1/3 of estate to surviving spouse if surviving children or descendants of children; 1/2 of estate to surviving spouse if surviving parents, siblings or children of siblings, but no surviving children.
Florida	Florida Statutes Annotated, §§731.005 et seq.	100% to surviving spouse if no surviving lineal descendants; $20,000 plus 1/2 of estate to surviving spouse if surviving children; 1/2 of estate to surviving spouse if decedent survived by a lineal descendant who is not a lineal descendant of surviving spouse.
Georgia	Georgia Statutes, Title 53, §§53-1-1 et seq.	100% to surviving spouse if no surviving children or their descendants; child's share to surviving spouse if surviving children or their descendants; 1/5 to surviving spouse if more than five surviving children or their descendants except surviving husband always takes a child's share.
Hawaii	Hawaii Revised Statutes, §§560 et seq.	100% to surviving spouse if no surviving children or parents; 1/2 of estate to surviving spouse if surviving children or parent.

APPENDIX 5

STATE	APPLICABLE STATUTE	BASIC INHERITANCE RULES
Idaho	Idaho Code, §§15-1-101 et seq.	1/2 of community property to surviving spouse with balance distributed to decedent's surviving descendants according to statute; 100% of separate property estate to surviving spouse if no surviving children or parents; $50,000 plus 1/2 of separate property estate to surviving spouse if surviving children and all are issue of surviving spouse; 1/2 of separate property estate to surviving spouse if surviving children and all not issue of surviving spouse; $50,000 plus 1/2 of separate property estate to surviving spouse if surviving parents but no surviving children.
Illinois	Illinois Annotated Statutes, Chapter 110, §§1-1 et seq.	100% to surviving spouse if no surviving descendants; 1/2 of estate to surviving spouse if surviving descendants; 100% to surviving descendants if no spouse; if no surviving spouse or descendants then entire estate to surviving parents, siblings or descendants of siblings in equal share except if there is only one surviving parent he or she takes both parents share.
Indiana	Indiana Statutes Annotated, §§29-1-1 et seq.	100% to surviving spouse if no surviving children, descendants of children, or parents; 1/2 of estate to surviving spouse if surviving children or descendants of children.
Iowa	Iowa Code Annotated, §§633.1 et seq.	If no surviving children, surviving spouse receives 1/2 of real property, 100% of exempt personal property, and 1/2 of personal property after debts, but all must equal at least $50,000; if surviving children, surviving spoouse receives 1/3 of real property, 100% of exempt personal property, and 1/2 of personal property after debts, but all must equal at least $50,000.
Kansas	Kansas Statutes Annotated, §§59-101	100% to surviving spouse if no surviving children or issue of deceased children; 1/2 of estate to surviving spouse if surviving children or issue of deceased children; if no surviving children, issue of deceased children or surviving spouse, 100% to surviving parents.
Kentucky	Kentucky Revised Statutes, §§391.010 et seq.	100% to surviving spouse if no surviving children, issue of deceased children, surviving parents or siblings; 1/2 of personal property, fee estate in 1/2 of real estate and life estate in real estate to surviving spouse if surviving children, issue of deceased children, surviving parents or siblings; $7,500.00 to surviving spouse or surviving infant child.

STATE	APPLICABLE STATUTE	BASIC INHERITANCE RULES
Louisiana	Louisiana Civil Code Annotated, Article 1470 et seq.	100% of community property if no surviving direct descendants; 1/2 of community property to surviving spouse if any surviving direct descendants.
Maine	Maine Revised Statutes Annotated, Title 18A, §§1-101 et seq.	100% to surviving spouse if no surviving children or parents; $50,000 plus 1/2 of estate to surviving spouse if surviving children and all are issue of surviving spouse; 1/2 of estate to surviving spouse if surviving children and all not issue of surviving spouse; $50,000 plus 1/2 of estate to surviving spouse if surviving parents but no surviving children.
Maryland	Annotated Code of Maryland, Estates and Trusts Section	100% to surviving spouse if no surviving children or parents; $15,000 plus 1/2 of estate to surviving spouse if surviving children; 1/2 of estate to surviving spouse if surviving minor children; $15,000 plus 1/2 of estate to surviving spouse if surviving parents but no surviving children.
Massachusetts	Massachusetts General Laws Annotated, Chapter 190, §§1 et seq.	100% to surviving spouse if no surviving children and estate does not exceed $50,000; If the estate exceeds $50,000 then $50,000 plus 1/2 of estate to surviving spouse; 1/2 of personal and real property to surviving spouse if surviving children.
Michigan	Michigan Comp. Laws Annotated, §§700.1 et seq.	100% to surviving spouse if no surviving children or parents; $60,000 plus 1/2 of estate to surviving spouse if surviving children and all are issue of surviving spouse; 1/2 of estate to surviving spouse if surviving children and all not issue of surviving spouse; $60,000 plus 1/2 of estate to surviving spouse if surviving parent and no surviving children.
Minnesota	Minnesota Statutes Annotated, Chapters 524; 525 and 527	100% to surviving spouse if no surviving children; $70,000 plus 1/2 of estate to surviving spouse if surviving children and all are issue of surviving spouse; 1/2 of estate to surviving spouse if surviving children and all not issue of surviving spouse.
Mississippi	Mississippi Code Annotated, §§91-1-1 et seq.	100% to surviving spouse if no surviving children or their descendants; if surviving children or their descendants, surviving spouse receives a child's share; children take in equal parts.

APPENDIX 5

STATE	APPLICABLE STATUTE	BASIC INHERITANCE RULES
Missouri	Missouri Statutes Annotated, §§474.010 et seq.	100% to surviving spouse if no surviving children or parents; $20,000 plus 1/2 of estate to surviving spouse if surviving children and all are issue of surviving spouse; 1/2 of estate to surviving spouse if surviving children and all not issue of surviving spouse; $20,000 plus 1/2 of estate to surviving spouse if surviving parents but no surviving children.
Montana	Montana Code Annotated, §§72-2-202 et seq.	100% to surviving spouse if no surviving children or if all surviving children are issue of surviving spouse; 1/2 of estate to surviving spouse if one surviving child not the issue of surviving spouse; 1/3 of estate to surviving spouse if more than one surviving child not the issue of surviving spouse.
Nebraska	Revised Statutes of Nebraska, §§30-101 et seq.	100% to surviving spouse if no surviving children or parents; $50,000 plus 1/2 of estate to surviving spouse if surviving children and all are issue of surviving spouse; 1/2 of estate to surviving spouse if surviving children and all not issue of surviving spouse; $50,000 plus 1/2 of estate to surviving spouse if surviving parents but no surviving children.
Nevada	Nevada Revised Statutes, Title 12, §§133.010 et seq.	100% of community property to surviving spouse; 1/2 of separate property to surviving spouse if one surviving child or child's descendants; 1/3 of separate property to surviving spouse if more than one surviving child or their descendants; 1/2 of separate property to surviving spouse if surviving parents but no surviving children or their descendants; 1/2 of separate property to surviving spouse if surviving siblings but no surviving children or their descendants, or surviving parents.
New Hampshire	New Hampshire Revised Statutes Annotated, Chapter 551.1 et seq.	100% to surviving spouse if no surviving children or parents; $50,000 plus 1/2 of estate to surviving spouse if surviving children and all are issue of surviving spouse; 1/2 of estate to surviving spouse if surviving children and all not issue of surviving spouse; $50,000 plus 1/2 of estate to surviving spouse if surviving parents but no surviving children.

STATE	APPLICABLE STATUTE	BASIC INHERITANCE RULES
New Jersey	Section 3B:3-1 et seq., of the New Jersey Statutes Annotated, §§3B: 3-1 et seq.	100% to surviving spouse if no surviving children or parents; $50,000 plus 1/2 of estate to surviving spouse if surviving children and all are issue of surviving spouse; 1/2 of estate to surviving spouse if surviving children and all not issue of surviving spouse; $50,000 plus 1/2 of estate to surviving spouse if surviving parents but no surviving children.
New Mexico	New Mexico Statutes Annotated, §§45-1-101 et seq.	100% to surviving spouse if no surviving children; 100% of community property and 1/4 of separate property to surviving spouse if surviving children.
New York	Consolidated Laws of New York Annotated, EPTL §§1-1.1 et seq.	$4,000 of personal property plus 1/2 of remaining personal property to surviving spouse if one surviving child or issue of deceased child; $4,000 of personal property plus 1/3 of remaining personal property to surviving spouse if more than one surviving child; $25,000 plus 1/2 of estate to surviving spouse if surviving parents but no surviving children.
North Carolina	General Statutes of North Carolina, §§28-A-1 et seq.	100% to surviving spouse if no surviving children or their descendants, or surviving parents; 1/2 of all real property and first $15,000 of personal property plus 1/2 of balance of personal property to surviving spouse if one surviving child or descendant of child; 1/3 of all real property and first $15,000 of personal property plus 1/3 of balance of personal property if surviving children or descendants of children; 1/2 of real property and first $15,000 of personal property plus 1/2 of balance of personal property if surviving parents but no surviving children or descendants of children.
North Dakota	North Dakota Code, §§30.1-08-01 et seq.	100% to surviving spouse if no surviving children or parents; $50,000 plus 1/2 of estate to surviving spouse if surviving children and all are issue of surviving spouse; 1/2 of estate to surviving spouse if surviving children and all not issue of surviving spouse; $50,000 plus 1/2 of estate to surviving spouse if surviving parents but no surviving children.

APPENDIX 5

STATE	APPLICABLE STATUTE	BASIC INHERITANCE RULES
Ohio	Ohio Revised Code Annotated, §§2105 et seq.	$60,000 plus 1/2 of estate to surviving spouse if one surviving child or descendant of deceased child, if child is issue of surviving spouse; $20,000 plus 1/2 of estate to surviving spouse if one surviving child or descendant of deceased child, if child is not issue of surviving spouse; $60,000 plus 1/3 of estate to surviving spouse if surviving children or descendants of deceased children, and all are issue of surviving spouse; $20,000 plus 1/3 of estate to surviving spouse if surviving children or descendants of children, and all are not issue of surviving spouse.
Oklahoma	Oklahoma Statutes Annotated, Title 84, §1-308	100% to surviving spouse if no surviving children, parents or siblings; 100% of joint property plus 1/3 of balance of estate if surviving parents or siblings but no surviving children; 1/2 of joint property and child's share of balance of estate if surviving children or descendants of children and all not issue of surviving spouse.
Oregon	Oregon Revised Statutes, §§112.015 et seq.	100% to surviving spouse if no surviving children; 1/2 of estate to surviving spouse if surviving children.
Pennsylvania	Pennsylvania Statutes Annotated, Title 20, §§101 et seq.	100% to surviving spouse if no surviving children or parents; $30,000 plus 1/2 of estate to surviving spouse if surviving children and all are issue of surviving spouse; 1/2 of estate to surviving spouse if surviving children and all not issue of surviving spouse; $30,000 plus 1/2 of estate to surviving spouse if surviving parents but no surviving children.
Rhode Island	General Laws of Rhode Island, §§33-1-1 et seq.	All real property to surviving spouse for life subject to any encumbrances; 100% of entire estate to surviving spouse if no surviving children or kindred; $50,000 plus 1/2 of personal property to surviving spouse if surviving kindred but no surviving children; 1/2 of personal property to surviving spouse if surviving children.
South Carolina	Code of Laws of South Carolina, §§21-1-10 et seq.	100% to surviving spouse if no surviving children or their descendants, parents, or siblings; 1/2 of estate to surviving spouse if one surviving child; 1/3 of estate to surviving spouse if more than one surviving child.

STATE	APPLICABLE STATUTE	BASIC INHERITANCE RULES
South Dakota	South Dakota Comp. Laws Annotated, §§29-1-1 et seq.	1/2 of estate to surviving spouse if one surviving child or descendant of deceased child; 1/3 of estate to surviving spouse if more than one surviving child, or one surviving child and surviving descendants of deceased children; 100% of estate to surviving children or descendants of deceased children if no surviving spouse; $100,000 plus 1/2 of balance of estate to surviving spouse if surviving parents, siblings or descendants of siblings, but no surviving children.
Tennessee	Tennessee Code Annotated, §§30-101 et seq.	100% to surviving spouse if no surviving children or their descendants; child's share not less than 1/3 of estate to surviving spouse if surviving children or their descendants.
Texas	Texas Probate Code, §§1 et seq.	100% of community property to surviving spouse if no surviving children or their descendants; 1/2 of community property to surviving spouse if surviving children or their descendants; 100% of personal property and 1/2 of real property to surviving spouse if no surviving children or their descendants with balance to decedent's other surviving relatives; 1/3 of personal property and a life estate in 1/3 of real property to surviving spouse if surviving children or their descendants.
Utah	Utah Code, §§75-1-101 et seq.	100% to surviving spouse if no surviving children or parents; $50,000 plus 1/2 of estate to surviving spouse if surviving children and all are issue of surviving spouse; 1/2 of estate to surviving spouse if surviving children and all not issue of surviving spouse; $100,000 plus 1/2 of estate to surviving spouse if surviving parents but no surviving children.
Vermont	Vermont Statutes Annotated, Title 14, §§1 et seq.	Surviving spouse takes dower or curtesy equal to 1/3 of real property; If no surviving children, surviving spouse inherits $25,000 plus 1/2 of remainder; if decedent leaves no surviving kindred, surviving spouse inherits the entire estate; if decedent leaves surviving children, surviving spouse's share limited to dower or curtesy.
Virginia	Code of Virginia, §§64.1 et seq.	All personal and real property in fee simple to surviving spouse unless decedent survived by children or their descendants who are not children of surviving spouse in which case 1/3 of personal and real property to surviving spouse and 2/3 to decedent's surviving children and their descendants.

APPENDIX 5

STATE	APPLICABLE STATUTE	BASIC INHERITANCE RULES
Washington	Revised Code of Washington Annotated, §§11.02.005 et seq.	100% of community property to surviving spouse; 1/2 of separate property to surviving spouse if surviving children; 3/4 of separate property to surviving spouse if surviving parents or siblings; 100% of separate property to surviving spouse if no surviving children, parents or siblings.
West Virginia	West Virginia Code, §§41-1-1 et seq.	Dower interest of 1/3 of all real property as life estate to surviving spouse; 1/3 of all personal property to surviving spouse if surviving children or their descendants; 100% of all personal property and real property to surviving spouse if no surviving children or their descendants.
Wisconsin	Wisconsin Statutes Annotated, §§852.01 et seq.	100% of estate to surviving spouse if no surviving children; first $25,000 plus 1/2 of balance of estate to surviving spouse if one surviving child of the marriage, or children of a deceased child of the marriage; first $25,000 plus 1/3 of balance of estate to surviving spouse if more than one surviving child of the marriage, or children of deceased child of the marriage; 1/2 of the estate to surviving spouse if surviving children not of the marriage, or children of a deceased child not of the marriage.
Wyoming	Wyoming Statutes Annotated, §§2-1-101 et seq.	100% to surviving spouse if no surviving children or their descendants; 1/2 of estate to surviving spouse if surviving children and their descendants; 1/2 of estate to surviving spouse if surviving parents or siblings, but no surviving children or their descendants.

APPENDIX 6:

SAMPLE PROBATE PETITION

```
                                        For Office Use Only
                              (Filing Fee Paid $ _____ )
                              ( _____ Certs: $ _____ )
                              ( $ _____ Bond, Fee: $ _____ )
                              (Receipt No: _____ No: _____ )
```

DO NOT LEAVE ANY ITEMS BLANK

SURROGATE'S COURT OF THE STATE OF NEW YORK
COUNTY OF
.... X
ADMINISTRATION PROCEEDING
Estate of
a/k/a

                                    Deceased.
.... X

PETITION FOR LETTERS OF:
[ ] Administration
[ ] Limited Administration
[ ] Administration with Limitations
[ ] Temporary Administration

File No. _____

TO THE SURROGATE'S COURT, County of

It is respectfully alleged:

1. The name, domicile and interest in this proceeding of the petitioner, who is of full age, is as follows:

Name: _____

Domicile: _____
              (Street Address)   (City/Town/Village)

    (County)   (State)   (Zip)   (Telephone Number)

Mailing address is: _____
                       (if different from domicile)

Citizenship (check one): [ ] U.S.A   [ ] Other (specify) _____

Interest of Petitioner (check one):

[ ] Distributee of decedent (state relationship) _____

[ ] Other (specify) _____

Is proposed Administrator an attorney? [ ] Yes [ ] No [If yes, submit statement pursuant to 22 NYCRR 207.19(g); see also 207.60 (Accounting of attorney-fiduciary).]

2. The name, domicile, date and place of death, and national citizenship of the above-named decedent are as follows [**The Death Certificate must be filed with this proceeding.** If the decedent's domicile is different from that shown on the death certificate, check box [ ] and attach an affidavit explaining the reason for this inconsistency.]:

Name: _____

Domicile: _____
             (Street Number)   (City, Village/Town)

         (State)   (Zip Code)

Township of: _____ County of: _____

Date of Death: _____ Place of Death: _____

Citizenship: (check one): [ ] U.S.A. [ ] Other (specify) _____

[Note: For Items 3a through c: Do not include any assets that are jointly held, held in trust for another, or have a named beneficiary.]

3. (a) The estimated gross value of the decedent's personal property passing by intestacy is less than $ _____ .

(b) The estimated gross value of the decedent's real property, in this state, which is [ ] improved, [ ] unimproved, passing by intestacy is less than $ _____ .

A brief description of each parcel is as follows:

(c) The estimated gross rent for a period of eighteen (18) months is the sum of $ _____ .

(d) In addition to the value of the personal property stated in paragraph (3) the following right of action existed on behalf of the decedent and survived his/her death, or is granted to the administrator of the decedent by special provision of law, and it is impractical to give a bond sufficient to cover the probable amount to be recovered therein: [Write "NONE" or state briefly the cause of action and the person against whom it exists, including names and carrier].

(e) If decedent is survived by a spouse and a parent, or parents but no issue, and there is a claim for wrongful death, check here [ ] and furnish name(s) and address(es) of parent(s) in Paragraph 7. See EPTL 5-4.4.

4. A diligent search and inquiry, including a search of any safe deposit box, has been made for a will of the decedent and none has been found. Petitioner(s) (has) (have) been unable to obtain any information concerning any will of the decedent and therefore allege(s), upon information and belief, that the decedent died without leaving any last will.

5. A search of the records of this Court shows that no application has ever been made for letters of administration upon the estate of the decedent or for the probate of a will of the decedent, and your petitioner is informed and verily believes that no such application ever has been made to the Surrogate's Court of any other county of this state.

6. The decedent left surviving the following who would inherit his/her estate pursuant to EPTL 4-1.1 and 4-1.2:

   a. [ ] Spouse (husband/wife). [If the decedent was divorced, see Uniform Court Rule 207.50].

   b. [ ] Child or children or descendants of predeceased child or children. [Must include marital, nonmarital, and adopted].

   c. [ ] Any issue of the decedent adopted by persons related to the decedent (DRL Section 117).

   d. [ ] Mother/Father.

   e. [ ] Sisters or brothers, either of whole or half blood, and issue of predeceased sisters or brothers.

   f. [ ] Grandmother/Grandfather.

   g. [ ] Aunts or uncles, and children of predeceased aunts and uncles (first cousins).

   h. [ ] First cousins once removed (children of first cousins).

[Information is required only as to those classes of surviving relatives who would take the property of decedent pursuant to EPTL 4-1.1. State "number" of survivors in each class. Insert "No" in all prior classes. Insert "X" in all subsequent classes].

APPENDIX 6

7. The decedent left surviving the following distributees, or other necessary parties, whose names, degrees of relationship, domiciles, post office addresses and citizenship are as follows:

[Note: Show clearly how each person is related to decedent. If relationship is through an ancestor who is deceased, give name, date of death, and relationship of the ancestor to the decedent. Use rider sheet if space in paragraph (7) is not sufficient. See Uniform Rules 207.16(b).
If any person listed in paragraph (7) is an nonmarital person, or descended from a nonmarital person, attach a copy of the order of filiation or Schedule A. If any person listed in paragraph (7) was adopted by any persons related by blood or marriage to decedent or descended from such persons, attach Schedule B.].

7a. The following are of full age and under no disability: [If nonmarital or adopted-out person, so indicate by attaching Schedule A and/or B]

Name	Relationship	Domicile and Mailing Address	Citizenship

7b. The following are infants and/or persons under disability: [Attach applicable Schedule A, B, C and/or D]

Name	Relationship	Domicile and Mailing Address	Citizenship

8. There are no outstanding debts or funeral expenses, except: [Write "NONE" or state same]

9. There are no other persons interested in this proceeding other than those hereinbefore mentioned.

WHEREFORE, your petitioner respectfully prays that: [Check and complete all relief requested]

( ) a. process issue to all necessary parties to show cause why letters should not be issued as requested;

( ) b. an order be granted dispensing with service of process upon those persons named in Paragraph (7) who have a right to letters prior or equal to that of the person nominated, and who are non-domiciliaries or whose names or whereabouts are unknown and cannot be ascertained;

( ) c. a decree award Letters of:

[ ] Administration to _____
[ ] Limited Administration to _____
[ ] Administration with Limitation to _____
[ ] Temporary Administration to _____

or to such other person or persons having a prior right as may be entitled thereto, and;

( ) d. That the authority of the representative under the foregoing Letters be limited with respect to the prosecution or enforcement of a cause of action on behalf of the estate, as follows: the administrator(s) may not enforce a judgment or receive any funds without further order of the Surrogate.

( ) e. That the authority of the representative under the foregoing Letters be limited as follows:

( ) f. [State any other relief requested].

Dated: _____

1. _____   2. _____
     (Signature of Petitioner)   (Signature of Petitioner)

   _____   _____
          (Print Name)   (Print Name)

APPENDIX 7:

SAMPLE NOTICE OF PROBATE

UF Form P-20 (Rev. 1/88)

State of New York

Surrogate's Court County of the Bronx

Probate Proceeding, Will of	**Notice of Probate**
....	File No. _____ 19____
Deceased	

Notice is hereby given that the Last Will and Testament of ...., late of the County of Bronx and State of New York, dated the .... day of .... ,19.........., has been offered for probate in the Surrogate's Court of the County of The Bronx, and that the proponent ..... of said will is ....

residing at ....
....

and that the following are the names and the post-office addresses of each person named or referred to in the said Will as substitute or successor executor(trix), trustee, guardian, legatee, devisee or other beneficiary, as set forth in the petition herein, who has not been cited or has not appeared or waived citation; that as to such persons as are infants or incompetents, the names and post-office addresses of the persons to whom an additional copy of the Notice of Probate is required to be mailed are shown; and opposite the name of each person is a characterization whether he/she is referred to in said Will as testamentary trustee or as guardian or as substitute or successor executor(trix) or as beneficiary.

Name	Post-Office Address	Nature of Interest or Status

Dated, ..., 19........

....
Attorney for Petitioner

Office and Post Office Address ....

STATE OF NEW YORK }
COUNTY OF } ss.:

...., residing at ....,
...., being duly sworn, says that he is over the age of .... years, that on the .... day of .... 19........., he deposited in a post office or in a post-office box regularly maintained by the United States Postal Service in the .... of .... State of New York, a copy of the foregoing Notice of Probate contained in a securely closed, post-paid wrapper directed to each of the above named persons, at the places set opposite their respective names.

Sworn to before me this .... day
of ...., 19.........

....
....
Notary Public

APPENDIX 8:

SAMPLE COURT ORDER ISSUING LETTERS TESTAMENTARY

P-17 (1/88)

At a Surrogate's Court, held in and for the County of Bronx, at the Bronx County Building, in the Borough of The Bronx, City of New York, on the   day of   19

PRESENT:

Hon. LEE L. HOLZMAN, Surrogate

IN THE MATTER OF PROVING THE LAST WILL AND TESTAMENT OF

No. .... P-19.........

Deceased.

Upon reading and filing the petition of

verified the   day of   , 19   , and a citation having been duly issued, served, waived, published and returned, herein, the allegations of the parties appearing having been heard, and the proofs having been duly taken by the Surrogate, pursuant to Section 1406 of the SCPA, among other things as to the execution of said instrument   , bearing date the   day of   , 19

Note Appearances

and the probate of said Will not having been contested,

and it appearing to the Surrogate that the Will was duly executed, and that the testa   , at the time of executing it, was in all respects competent to make a Will and not under restraint:

It is Ordered, Adjudged and Decreed, that the instrument offered for probate herein be and the same hereby is   admitted to probate as the Last Will and Testament of the said Deceased, valid to pass real and personal property, and that letters testamentary be issued thereon to the execut   who may qualify thereunder.

Enter:

Surrogate

APPENDIX 9:

STATE LAW EXCEPTIONS TO CONVENTIONAL PROBATE

STATE	APPLICABLE STATUTE	PROBATE EXEMPTION	SIMPLIFIED PROBATE
Alabama	Alabama Code, Title 43, Chapter 2, §§690, et seq.	Not Available	Yes - up to $3,000 of personal property
Alaska	Alaska Statutes, Title 13, Chapter 6, §13.16.08	Not Available	Yes - no dollar limit
Arizona	Arizona Revised Statutes, §§14-3971, et seq.	Yes - up to $30,000 of personal property	Not available, except for certain types of family property
Arkansas	Arkansas Statutes Annotate, §§G2.2127, et seq.	Yes - up to $25,000	Not available
California	California Probate Code, §§13200, et seq.	Yes - up to $60,000 of personal property and real property interest, $10,000	No dollar limit to surviving spouse on community property petition
Colorado	Colorado Revised Statutes, §§15-12-1201	Yes - up to $20,000 of net estate	Not available except for certain types of family property
Connecticut	Connecticut General Statutes Annotated, Title 45, §§266 et seq.	Not Available	Yes - Up to $10,000 to spouse, next of kin, or creditor
Delaware	Delaware Code Annotated, Title 12, §2306 et seq.	Yes - up to $12,500 of personal property to spouse, grandparents, children or other statutory relative	Not Available
District of Columbia	District of Columbia Code, Title 20, §§2101 et seq.	Not Available	Yes - up to $10,000 of personal property

PROBATE LAW

STATE	APPLICABLE STATUTE	PROBATE EXEMPTION	SIMPLIFIED PROBATE
Florida	Florida Statutes Annotated, §§735.103 et seq.; 735.201 et seq.; and 735.301 et seq.	Not Available	Yes -Up to $25,000 of Florida property and up to $60,000 of estate to family members
Georgia	None	Not Available	Not Available
Hawaii	Hawaii Revised Statutes, §§560:3-1205 et seq.; and 560:3-1213	Yes - up to $2,000	Yes - up to $20,000 of Hawaii property
Idaho	Idaho Code, §15-3-301 et seq.	Not Available	Yes -no dollar limit
Illinois	Illinois Annotated Statutes, Chapter 110-1/2, §§6-8 et seq.; 9-8 et seq.; and 25-1 et seq.	Yes - up to $25,000 of personal property; or if all beneficiaries are Illinois residents and are in agreement and no state of federal estate taxes are due	Yes - up to $50,000
Indiana	Indiana Statutes Annotated, §§27-1-7.5-5 et seq.; and 29-1-8-2 et seq.	Yes - up to $8,500 of personal property	Yes - no dollar limit
Iowa	Iowa Code Annotated, §635 et seq.	Not Available	Yes -up to $15,000 of total value of Iowa property to surviving spouse, minor children or parents only
Kansas	Kansas Statutes Annotated, §§59-3201 et seq.; and 59-3301 et seq.	Not Available	Yes - no dollar limit
Kentucky	Kentucky Revised Statutes, §§391.030 et seq. and 395.450 et seq.	Not Available	Yes - by agreement of all beneficiaries or when estate to spouse is under $7,500

APPENDIX 9

STATE	APPLICABLE STATUTE	PROBATE EXEMPTION	SIMPLIFIED PROBATE
Louisiana	No applicable statute	Not Available	Only if resident dies intestate with estate under $50,000
Maine	Maine Revised Statutes Annotated, Title 18A, §1-101	Not Available	Yes - no dollar limit
Maryland	Annotated Code of Maryland, §§5-601 et seq.	Not available	Yes - up to $20,000
Massachusetts	Massachusetts General Laws Annotated, Chapter 195, §§16 et seq.	Not Available	Yes - up to $15,000 of personal property
Michigan	Michigan Comp. Laws Annotated, §§9.1936; 27.5101 et seq.; and 257.236	Not available	Yes - up to $5,000
Minnesota	Minnesota Statutes Annotated, §§525.51 et seq.	Not Available	Yes - up to $30,000
Mississippi	Mississippi Code Annotated, §91-7-147	Not Available	Yes - up to $500
Missouri	Missouri Statutes Annotated, §5-473.097	Not Available	Yes - up to $15,000
Montana	Montana Code Annotated, Title 72, §§3-201 et seq.	Not Available	Yes - up to $15,000
Nebraska	Revised Statutes of Nebraska, §§30-2414 et seq.	Not Available	Yes - no dollar limit
Nevada	Nevada Revised Statutes, §§145.070 et seq. and 146.010 et seq.	Yes - up to $25,000	Yes - up to $100,000

STATE	APPLICABLE STATUTE	PROBATE EXEMPTION	SIMPLIFIED PROBATE
New Hampshire	New Hampshire Revised Statutes Annotated, Chapter 553,331 et seq.	Not Available except up to $500 to surviving spouse	Yes - up to $5,000
New Jersey	No applicable statute	Not available except $10,000 to spouse and $5,000 to others if resident dies intestate	Not Available
New Mexico	New Mexico Statutes, §§45-3-1202 and 45-3-1204	Yes - up to $5,000	Yes - up to $10,000
New York	Consolidated Laws of New York Annotated, EPTL §§1301 et seq.	Yes - up to $10,000 and certain exempt property	Not Available
North Carolina	General Statutes of North Carolina, Chapter 28A, §25-1.1	Yes - up to $10,000 personal property	Not Available
North Dakota	North Dakota Code, §§30.1-14 et seq.	Not Available	Yes - no dollar limit
Ohio	Ohio Revised Code Annotated, §2113.02	Not Available	Yes - up to $15,000
Oklahoma	Oklahoma Statutes Annotated, Title 58, §§241 et seq.	Not Available	Yes -up to $60,000
Oregon	Oregon Revised Statutes, §§114.515 et seq.	Yes -up to $15,000 personal property and $35,000 real property	Not Available
Pennsylvania	Pennsylvania Statutes Annotated, Title 20, §§3102 et seq.	Not Available	Yes - up to $10,000 personal property
Rhode Island	No applicable statute	Not Available	Not Available

APPENDIX 9

STATE	APPLICABLE STATUTE	PROBATE EXEMPTION	SIMPLIFIED PROBATE
South Carolina	Code of Laws of South Carolina, Title 62, Chapter 3, §§1201 and 1203 et seq.	Yes - up to $10,000	Yes -up to $10,000
South Dakota	South Dakota Codified Laws, §§30-11A et seq.; and 30-11-1	Yes - up to $5,000	Yes - up to $60,000
Tennessee	Tennessee Code Annotated, Title 30, Chapter 4, §§101 et seq.	Not Available	Yes - up to $10,000 real property
Texas	Texas Probate Code, §§137 et seq. and 145 et seq.	Yes -up to $50,000	Yes - no dollar limit
Utah	Utah Code, Title 75, §3-301	Not Available	Yes - no dollar limit
Vermont	Vermont Statutes Annotated, Title 14, §§1901 et seq.	Not Available	Yes -up to $10,000 personal property
Virginia	Code of Virginia, §§64.1-132 et seq.	Yes - up to $5,000 personal property and $5,000 wages or bank account	Not Available
Washington	Revised Code of Washington Annotated, Title 11, §§62.010 et seq.	Yes -up to $10,000 personal property	Not Available
West Virginia	West Virginia Code, Chapter 24, Article 2, §1	Not Available	Yes - up to $50,000
Wisconsin	Wisconsin Statutes Annotated, §§867.03 et seq. and 867.045 et seq.	Yes -up to $5,000 personal property	Yes - up to $10,000
Wyoming	Wyoming Statutes Annotated, §2-1-201	Yes - up to $30,000	Not Available

APPENDIX 10:

SAMPLE NEW YORK STATE SUCCESSION TAX RETURN

STATE OF CONNECTICUT
DEPARTMENT OF REVENUE SERVICES
INHERITANCE TAX DIVISION
P.O. Box 2972, Hartford, CT 06104-2972
Rev. 7/90)

Form S-1
SUCCESSION TAX RETURN

STATE TAX FILE NUMBER

- REFER TO INSTRUCTION BOOKLET WHILE COMPLETING THIS RETURN -

IDENTIFICATION

DECEDENT'S LAST NAME	DECEDENT'S FIRST NAME, MIDDLE INITIAL	ALSO KNOWN AS	
DECEDENT'S SOCIAL SECURITY NUMBER	DECEDENT'S DATE OF DEATH	DECEDENT'S DATE OF BIRTH	PROBATE COURT	P.C. DISTRICT #

DECEDENT'S HOME ADDRESS — WAS THE DECEDENT A CONNECTICUT RESIDENT? ☐ YES ☐ NO

TYPE OF ESTATE
☐ TESTATE ☐ INTESTATE ☐ TAX PURPOSES ONLY

IF TESTATE, WAS WILL ADMITTED TO PROBATE COURT? ☐ YES ☐ NO

IS THE ESTATE REQUIRED TO FILE A FEDERAL ESTATE TAX RETURN? ☐ YES ☐ NO (If "Yes," attach copy)

NAME OF PERSON(S) FILING RETURN
TITLE: ☐ EXECUTOR ☐ ADMINISTRATOR ☐ OTHER (Explain)

ADDRESS OF PERSON FILING RETURN — TELEPHONE NUMBER

ATTORNEY'S NAME & FIRM — TELEPHONE NUMBER

ATTORNEY'S ADDRESS

SCHEDULE 1 - BENEFICIARIES

Names of Beneficiaries and/or Transferees	Relationship to Decedent	Nature of Estate	Date of Birth	Estimation of Net Taxable Estate passing to Recipient
				$

DECEASED BENEFICIARIES NAMED IN THE WILL AND TRUST(S):

Name	Date of Death	Name	Date of Death

Affidavit(s)

STATE OF — COUNTY OF — DATE

The undersigned, being duly sworn, make affidavit and say that, to the best of their knowledge and belief, this return is a true and complete statement of the gross taxable estate of the above-named decedent, of the deductions applicable thereto, and of the beneficiaries thereof, as required by the statutes of the State of Connecticut.

NAME OF AFFIANT (Type or Print)	SIGNATURE	TITLE (Executor, Administrator, Survivor, Donee)

Subscribed and sworn to before me on the above date. | SIGNATURE | TITLE (Comm. Sup. Ct., Notary Public, Judge, Clerk)

CERTIFICATION TO COMMISSIONER OF REVENUE SERVICES (For Probate Court Use Only)

The within and foregoing is a true and attested copy of the tax return on file with the probate court for the district named below.

DISTRICT OF	DATE	SIGNATURE	Judge Clerk Asst. Clerk

PROBATE COURT SEAL

CERTIFICATE OF OPINION OF NO TAX (For Probate Court Use Only) TO BE USED IF NO TAX IS DUE

APPORTIONMENT BY CLASS	AA $	A $	B $	C $	Exempt $

REMARKS:

I have examined this return and have calculated, as shown above, the taxable value of transfers reported herein for each class of beneficiary. I find that this value is less for each class than the exemption applicable to that class. In my opinion, therefore, there will be no succession tax due on account of transfers reported on this return and I so certify.

DATE — SIGNED (Judge)

SCHEDULE 2 - GENERAL QUESTIONS

1a. Cause of decedent's death: _____ 1b. Length of last illness _____

2. Decedent's Physicians (Names and Addresses)
_____
_____

3. Hospitals and Convalescent Homes: (Names and Addresses) in which decedent was confined within 3 years of death (if applicable).
_____
_____
_____

4. Marital status at time of death:

    4a. ☐ Married   4b. ☐ Widow(er) - Name and date of death of deceased spouse _____

    4c. ☐ Divorced   4d. ☐ Single   4e. ☐ Legally separated

Did the decedent at the time of death own or have any interest in any of the following:	YES	NO	IF "YES" COMPLETE SCHEDULE
*5. Connecticut real property (real estate) other than such property held jointly with right of survivorship?			4
6. Stocks and bonds, including U.S. Savings Bonds, wherever located, other than such items held jointly with right of survivorship?			5
7. Mortgages, notes, cash, or bank accounts, wherever located, other than such items held jointly with right of survivorship.			6
8. Partnership or unincorporated business, wherever located?			6
9. Life insurance on the life of another?			6
*10. Personal property not mentioned in Questions 5 through 9 and not held jointly with right of survivorship?			6
11. Checking or savings accounts and U.S. Savings Bonds held jointly with right of survivorship? (Includes accounts in banks, building or savings and loan associations, or credit unions.)			7
*12. Connecticut real property (real estate) held jointly with right of survivorship?			8
*13. Personal property held jointly with right of survivorship and not mentioned in Question 11? (Includes joint stocks or bonds, but not U.S. Savings Bonds.)			8
14. Annuity; pension, stock-bonus or profit-sharing plan; retirement annuity or other plan under which the estate or a beneficiary has received or will receive a payment or payments as a result of decedent's death?			11

Did the decedent at any time during his/her life do any of the following:	YES	NO	IF "YES" COMPLETE SCHEDULE
*15. Make any gifts to another or others within 3 years prior to death?			10
*16. Transfer Connecticut real estate into a trust or create any trusts including trustee bank accounts, but excluding life insurance trusts funded only with life insurance policies?			10
*17. Make any transfers of property, real or personal, in which he retained any interest such as possession, use, income or enjoyment, or for which he received a private annuity?			10
*18. Make any transfers of property, including P.O.D. (payable on death) bonds, in such a manner that the transferee came into possession or enjoyment of same at or after the death of the decedent?			10
19. Possess a power to appoint, use, or withdraw all or a portion of the principal of a fund (including life insurance benefits) created by another?			9

	YES	NO	
20. Has any real estate, closely held security or unincorporated business interest listed on this return been sold, or is it under contract for sale? If yes, please provide details in appropriate schedule.			
21. Did the decedent and surviving spouse acquire assets together while living in a community property state, which assets were held in one spouse's name at decedent's death?			
22. Were any claimed deductions covered by insurance?			
23. Was a disclaimer filed in this estate? (If "Yes," please submit a copy of each disclaimer.)			
24. Are you claiming the Special Farmland Valuation?			4

*IF DECEDENT WAS NOT A RESIDENT, answer only the questions which have asterisks beside them in this schedule, and only as they apply to real property (real estate) or tangible personal property located in Connecticut.

Form S-1 (Rev. 7/90)   Page 2

APPENDIX 10

SCHEDULE 3 - RECAPITULATION & ESTIMATION OF TAX

RECAPITULATION

	ASSETS			VALUE OR AMOUNT CONCEDED TAXABLE
1.	Real Property Not Owned in Survivorship - **Schedule 4**		1	
2.	Stocks and Bonds Not Owned in Survivorship - **Total of Schedules 5A & 5B**		2	
3.	Miscellaneous Personal Property Not Owned in Survivorship - **Schedule 6**		3	
4.	Survivorship Bank Accounts and U.S. Savings Bonds			
	CONCEDED ENTIRELY TAXABLE - **Total of Schedules 7A & 7B**	4		
5.	CLAIMED FRACTIONALLY TAXABLE - **Schedule 7E**	5		
6.	TOTAL TAXABLE AMOUNT (Lines 4 & 5)		6	
7.	Other Survivorship Property			
	CONCEDED ENTIRELY TAXABLE - **Schedule 8A**	7		
8.	CLAIMED FRACTIONALLY TAXABLE - **Total of Sch. 8B & 8C**	8		
9.	TOTAL TAXABLE VALUE (Lines 7 & 8)		9	
10.	Powers of Appointment - **Schedule 9**		10	
11.	Transfers During Decedent's Lifetime - **Schedule 10**		11	
12.	Death Benefits, Annuities, Pensions, Retirement Benefits - **Schedule 11**		12	
13.	**GROSS TAXABLE ESTATE** (Sum of Schedules 4 through 11)		13	

DEDUCTIONS

	Schedule 12			
14.	A. Debts	14		
15.	B. Real Estate Taxes	15		
16.	C. Personal Property Taxes	16		
17.	D. Income Taxes	17		
18.	E. Special Assessments	18		
19.	F. Funeral Expenses	19		
20.	G. Cemetery Expenses	20		
21.	H. Fiduciaries' Fees	21		
22.	I. Attorney's Fees	22		
23.	J. Allowance for Spouse	23		
24.	K. Unpaid Mortgages	24		
25.	L. Administrative Expenses	25		
26.	**TOTAL DEDUCTIONS** (Sum of Schedules 12A - 12L)		26	
27.	**NET TAXABLE ESTATE** (Gross Estate less Deductions) (Line 13 minus Line 26)		27	

ESTIMATION OF TAX *(See Tax Table in Instructions)*

	Apportionment by Class:	Amount	Tax Due		
28.	Class AA				
29.	Class A				
30.	Class B				
31.	Class C				
32.	Exempt		- 0 -		
33.	Compromise, per 12-355				
34.	TOTAL (must equal Line 27)	$			
35.	Estimated Tax Due (Sum of Lines 28 through 33)			35	
36.	Estimated Interest Due			36	
37.	Estimated Total Tax and Interest Due (Sum of Lines 35 & 36)			37	
38.	Less Prior Payments			38	
39.	Estimated Balance / (Refund) Due (Line 37 minus Line 38)			39	

Form S-1 (Rev. 7/90)   Page 3

SCHEDULE 4 - Real Property Not Owned In Survivorship

ITEM NO.	DESCRIPTION	LOCAL ASSESSED VALUE AT DEATH	% OF DECEDENT'S INTEREST	FAIR MARKET VALUE OF DECEDENT'S INTEREST AT DEATH
1.		$		$
2.		$		$
3.		$		$
			TOTAL	$

SCHEDULE 5 - Stocks and Bonds Not Owned In Survivorship

SCHEDULE 5A - CLOSELY HELD SECURITIES

ITEM NO.	NUMBER OF SHARES	DESCRIPTION	% OF DECEDENT'S INTEREST	FAIR MARKET VALUE AT DEATH PER SHARE	TOTAL
1.			$	$	
				TOTAL	$

Form S-1 (Rev. 7/90)

APPENDIX 10

SCHEDULE 5 (continued) - Stocks and Bonds Not Owned in Survivorship

SCHEDULE 5B - MARKETABLE SECURITIES

ITEM NO.	NUMBER OF SHARES	DESCRIPTION	% OF DECEDENT'S INTEREST	FAIR MARKET VALUE AT DEATH	
				PER SHARE	TOTAL
1.				$	$
				TOTAL	$

SCHEDULE 6 - Miscellaneous Personal Property Not Owned in Survivorship

ITEM NO.	DESCRIPTION	FAIR MARKET VALUE AT DEATH
1.		$
	TOTAL	$

orm S-1 (Rev. 7/90)   Page 5

SCHEDULE 7 - SURVIVORSHIP BANK ACCOUNTS AND SAVINGS BONDS

PART I. BANK ACCOUNTS AND SAVINGS BONDS CONCEDED ENTIRELY TAXABLE

SCHEDULE 7A. Survivorship Bank Accounts Conceded Entirely Taxable

ITEM NUMBER	NAME OF BANK AND ACCOUNT NUMBER	NAME OF SURVIVOR & RELATIONSHIP TO DECEDENT	TOTAL AMOUNT AT DEATH
1.			$
		TOTAL	$

SCHEDULE 7B. Survivorship Savings Bonds Conceded Entirely Taxable

ITEM NUMBER	DESCRIPTION OF BONDS SERIES	# OF BONDS	NAME OF SURVIVOR & RELATIONSHIP TO DECEDENT	TOTAL FACE VALUE	TOTAL VALUE AT DEATH
1.				$	$
				TOTAL	$

Form S-1 (Rev. 7/90)

APPENDIX 10

SCHEDULE 7 (continued) - Survivorship Bank Accounts and Savings Bonds

PART II. BANK ACCOUNTS AND SAVINGS BONDS CLAIMED FRACTIONALLY TAXABLE
Schedules 7C and 7D are each continued through successive tables. Give each item the same item number throughout each table.

SCHEDULE 7C - SURVIVORSHIP BANK ACCOUNTS CLAIMED FRACTIONALLY TAXABLE

ITEM NO.	NAME OF BANK, ACCOUNT NO., and whether checking (C) or Savings (S)	YEAR MADE JOINT	% of Monetary Contribution to Each Account — Decedent	% of Monetary Contribution to Each Account — Survivor	TOTAL AMOUNT AT DEATH
1.					$
		TOTAL (Enter also on Schedule 7E)			$

Repeat Item Nos. from above	NAME OF SURVIVOR AND RELATIONSHIP TO DECEDENT	ADDRESS
1.		

Repeat Item Nos. from above	What was decedent's state of health when account was made joint?	Where was the passbook or proof of ownership kept?	Did survivor, during life of decedent, use any such funds for himself? YES/NO	IF "YES" — When	IF "YES" — How Much
1.					$

Repeat Item Nos. from above	Why was account created?	Whose social security number was used for the account?	Did decedent report all interest from account on his income tax return? YES/NO	IF "NO," EXPLAIN
1.				

Form S-1 (Rev. 7/90)   Page 7

SCHEDULE 7 (continued) - Survivorship Bank Accounts & Savings Bonds

SCHEDULE 7D - SURVIVORSHIP SAVINGS BONDS CLAIMED FRACTIONALLY TAXABLE

Item No.	Series	NO. OF BONDS	PERIOD OF TIME OVER WHICH BONDS PURCHASED	FACE VALUE	APPROX. % CONTRIBUTED BY DECEDENT	TOTAL VALUE AT DEATH
1.				$		$

TOTAL (Enter also on Schedule 7E) $

Repeat Item Nos. from above	NAME OF SURVIVOR AND RELATIONSHIP TO DECEDENT	ADDRESS
1.		

Repeat Item Nos. from above	What was decedent's state of health when bonds were placed in survivorship?	Where were bonds kept? If in a safe deposit box, in whose name was safe deposit box held?	Whose social security number was on the bonds?
1.			

Repeat Item Nos. from above	Were bonds income producing?	If "YES," who received the income from these bonds during decedent's lifetime?	Did decedent report all the income from these bonds on his income tax return?	
			YES/NO	IF "NO," Explain
1.				

SCHEDULE 7E - SUMMARY

From Schedule 7C. Survivorship Bank Accounts Claimed Fractionally Taxable *(Enter total amount)*	$
From Schedule 7D. Survivorship U.S. Savings Bonds Claimed Fractionally Taxable *(Enter total value)*	$
Subtotal	$
Less exemption	$ 5,000.00
Balance	$
FRACTIONAL PART OF BALANCE CONCEDED TAXABLE	$

Form S-1 (Rev. 7/90)

APPENDIX 10

SCHEDULE 8 - OTHER SURVIVORSHIP PROPERTY

SURVIVORSHIP PROPERTY CONCEDED ENTIRELY TAXABLE

SCHEDULE 8A. Survivorship Property (Real and Personal) Conceded Entirely Taxable

ITEM NUMBER	DESCRIPTION	NAME OF SURVIVOR & RELATIONSHIP TO DECEDENT	LOCAL ASSESSED VALUE AT DEATH	TOTAL AMOUNT AT DEATH
1.		$		$
			TOTAL	$

SURVIVORSHIP PROPERTY CLAIMED FRACTIONALLY TAXABLE

SCHEDULE 8B. Survivorship Real Property Claimed Fractionally Taxable

ITEM NUMBER	DESCRIPTION	LOCAL ASSESSED VALUE AT DEATH	TOTAL VALUE AT DATE OF DEATH	FRACTIONAL VALUE CONCEDED TAXABLE
1.		$	$	$
			TOTAL	$

Repeat Item Nos. from above	NAME AND RELATIONSHIP TO DECEDENT	ADDRESS	DATE SURVIVORSHIP CREATED
1.			

ANSWER ALL QUESTIONS REGARDING FRACTIONALLY TAXABLE REAL PROPERTY

Repeat Item Nos. from above	What % of purchase price was paid by		Did decedent have exclusive title to property before creation of survivorship?	To what extent was property used as a home?	Was property income producing?	IF "YES"		Did decedent report all such income from property on his income tax returns?	IF "NO," what % did he report?	DATE SURVIVORSHIP CREATED	DATE DEED RECORDED
	Decedent	Survivor				Did decedent receive all of income?	If not all, what % did he receive?				
1.	%	%		%			%		%		

Form S-1 (Rev. 7/90) Page 9

SCHEDULE 8 (continued) - Other Survivorship Property

SCHEDULE 8C - SURVIVORSHIP PERSONAL PROPERTY CLAIMED FRACTIONALLY TAXABLE

ITEM NO.	DESCRIPTION	TOTAL VALUE AT DATE OF DEATH	FRACTIONAL VALUE CONCEDED TAXABLE
1.		$	$
		TOTAL $	

Repeat Item Nos. from above	NAME AND RELATIONSHIP TO DECEDENT	ADDRESS	DATE SURVIVORSHIP CREATED
1.			

Repeat Item Nos. from above	Did decedent pay entire purchase price?	Was property income producing?	If "Yes," what % of such income did decedent receive?	Did decedent report all income from property on his income tax return?	If "NO," what % did he report?	Did decedent have exclusive title to property before creation of survivorship?
1.			%		%	

SCHEDULE 9 - POWERS OF APPOINTMENT

ITEM NO.	DESCRIPTION	TOTAL VALUE AT DEATH	AMOUNT CONCEDED TAXABLE
1.		$	$
		TOTAL	$

Form S-1 (Rev. 7/90)

APPENDIX 10

SCHEDULE 10 - TRANSFERS DURING DECEDENT'S LIFETIME

ITEM NO.	DESCRIPTION (If real estate, furnish local assessed value at death.)	NAME & RELATIONSHIP OF TRANSFEREE	TOTAL VALUE AT DATE OF DEATH	VALUE CONCEDED TAXABLE
1.			$	$
			TOTAL	$

SCHEDULE 11 - DEATH BENEFITS, ANNUITIES, PENSION PLANS, RETIREMENT BENEFITS

ITEM NO.	DESCRIPTION	TOTAL VALUE AT DEATH	AMOUNT CONCEDED TAXABLE
1.		$	$
		TOTAL	$

Repeat Item Nos. from above	NAME OF BENEFICIARY & RELATIONSHIP TO DECEDENT	IF PAID IN A LUMP SUM — AMOUNT, and was it entirely a return of retirement contributions (including accrued interest)?	IF NOT PAID IN A LUMP SUM — What were the amounts and terms of payment?	IF PAYABLE FOR LIFE — Beneficiary's Date of Birth
1.		$ YES/NO	$	

			IF AN EXCLUSION IS BEING CLAIMED, (complete the following)		
Repeat Item Nos. from above	Is this a "qualified plan" under the provisions of the Internal Revenue Code	AMOUNT OF DECEDENT'S CONTRIBUTIONS (incl. accrued interest)	AMOUNT OF EMPLOYER'S CONTRIBUTIONS (incl. accrued interest)	If Employer's Contributions Not Ascertainable — Had decedent retired before death? (If yes, give date of retirement)	If "YES," what were his and his beneficiary's benefits upon decedent's retirement?
1.		$	$		

Form S-1 (Rev. 7/90)   Page 11

SCHEDULE 12 - DEDUCTIONS

SCHEDULE 12A - DEBTS

Item No.	Claimant	Description of Claim	Date of Service and/or Period of Time Covered by Claim	Date of Payment	Amount
1.					$
				TOTAL	$

QUESTIONS REGARDING SCHEDULE 12A	YES (x)	NO (x)	DOES NOT APPLY (x)	QUESTIONS REGARDING SCHEDULE 12A	YES (x)	NO (x)	DOES NOT APPLY (x)
1. Were all debts listed incurred by decedent prior to death and paid after death?				3. Did decedent receive entire proceeds from loans and notes listed?			
2. Are all deductions for medical expenses net after hospitalization insurance, medicare, medicaid, etc.?				4. If a note or loan is secured by collateral, has the collateral been reported elsewhere on this return?			

SCHEDULE 12B - DECEDENT'S SHARE OF UNPAID TAXES ON REAL PROPERTY

Item No.	Address of Property (No., Street, Town)	Entire Local Assessed Value at Death	Assessment Date	Amount
1.		$		$
			TOTAL	$

Form S-1 (Rev. 7/90)

APPENDIX 10

SCHEDULE 12 (continued) - Deductions

SCHEDULE 12C - UNPAID TAXES ON PERSONAL PROPERTY

Item No.	Description	Town	Assessment Date	Amount
1.				$
			TOTAL	$

SCHEDULE 12D - DECEDENT'S SHARE OF UNPAID INCOME TAX

Item No.	Year	Decedent's Share
1.		$
	TOTAL	$

SCHEDULE 12E - SPECIAL ASSESSMENTS

Item No.	Address of Property	Nature of Assessment	Assessment Date	Amount
1.				$
			TOTAL	$

SCHEDULE 12F - FUNERAL EXPENSES

Item No.	Payee and Service Rendered	Gross Amount	Contributions	Net Amount
1.		$	$	$
			TOTAL	$

SCHEDULE 12G - CEMETERY EXPENSES

Item No.	Payee	In Consideration of	Amount
1.			$
		TOTAL	$

SCHEDULE 12H - EXECUTOR OR ADMINISTRATOR FEES

Name	Fee
	$
TOTAL	$

SCHEDULE 12I - ATTORNEYS' FEES

Name	Fee
	$
TOTAL	$

Form S-1 (Rev. 7/90)   Page 13

PROBATE LAW

SCHEDULE 12 (continued) - Deductions

SCHEDULE 12J - SUPPORT PAYMENTS

Item No.	Payee	In Consideration Of	Date of Birth (Other than spouse)	Period of Time Covered	Amount Paid
1.					$

TOTAL $

SCHEDULE 12K - UNPAID MORTGAGES

Item No.	Description	% of Decedent's Interest	Balance of Mortgage	Amount Claimed Deductible
1.				$

TOTAL $

SCHEDULE 12L - ADMINISTRATION EXPENSES

Item No.	Payee	In Consideration of	Date of service and/or period of time covered	Date of Payment	Amount
1.					$

TOTAL $

Form S-1 (Rev. 7/90)   Page 14

APPENDIX 11:

UNIFORM PROBATE CODE - TABLE OF CONTENTS

ARTICLE 1
General Provisions, Definitions and Probate Jurisdiction of Court

PART 1. Short Title, Construction, General Provisions

Section 1-101. Short Title

Section 1-102. Purposes: Rule of Construction

Section 1-103. Supplementary General Principles of Law Applicable

Section 1-104. Severability

Section 1-105. Construction Against Implied Repeal

Section 1-106. Effect of Fraud and Evasion

Section 1-107. Evidence as to Death or Status Acts by Holder of General Power

PART 2. Definitions

Section 2-101. General Definitions

PART 3. Scope, Jurisdiction and Courts

Section 1-301. Territorial Application

Section 1-302. Subject Matter Jurisdiction

Section 1-303. Venue; Multiple Proceedings; Transfer

Section 1-304. Practice in Court

Section 1-305. Records and Certified Copies

Section 1-306. Jury Trial

Section 1-307. Registrar; Powers

Section 1-308. Appeals

Section 1-309. Qualifications of Judge

Section 1-310. Oath or Affirmation on Filed Documents

PART 4. Notice, Parties and Representation in Estate, Litigation and Other Matters

Section 1-401. Notice; Method and Time of Giving

Section 1-402. Notice; Waiver

Section 1-403. Pleadings; When Parties Bound by Others; Notice

ARTICLE II
Intestate Succession and Wills

PART I. Intestate Succession

Section 2-101. Intestate Estate

Section 2-102. Share of the Spouse

Section 2-102A. Share of the Spouse

Section 2-103. Share of Heirs Other Than Surviving Spouse

Section 2-104. Requirement That Heir Survive Decedent For 120 Hours

Section 2-105. No Taker

Section 2-106. Representation

Section 2-107. Kindred of Half Blood

Section 2-108. Afterborn Heirs

Section 2-109. Meaning of Child and Related Terms

Section 2-110. Advancements

Section 2-111. Debts to Decedent

Section 2-112. Alienage

Section 2-113. Dower and Curtesy Abolished

PART 2. Elective Share of Surviving Spouse

Section 2-201. Right to Elective Share

Section 2-202. Augmented Estate

Section 2-203. Right of Election Personal to Surviving Spouse

Section 2-204. Waiver of Right to Elect and of Other Rights

Section 2-205. Proceeding for Elective Share; Time Limit

Section 2-206. Effect of Election on Benefits by Will or Statute

Section 2-207. Charging Spouse With Gifts Received; Liability of Others For Balance of Elective Share

PART 3. Spouse and Children Unprovided for in Wills

Section 2-301. Omitted Spouse

Section 2-302. Pretermitted Children

PART 4. Exempt Property and Allowances

Section 2-401. Homestead Allowance

Section 2-401A. Constitutional Homestead

Section 2-402. Exempt Property

Section 2-403. Family Allowance

Section 2-404. Source, Determination and Documentation

PART 5. Wills

Section 2-501. Who May Make a Will

Section 2-502. Execution

Section 2-503. Holographic Will

Section 2-504. Self-proved Will

Section 2-505. Who May Witness

Section 2-506. Choice of Law as to Execution

Section 2-507. Revocation by Writing or by Act

Section 2-508. Revocation by Divorce; No Revocation by Other Changes of Circumstances

Section 2-509. Revival of Revoked Will

Section 2-510. Incorporation by Reference

Section 2-511. Testamentary Additions to Trusts

Section 2-512. Events of Independent Significance

Section 2-513. Separate Writing Identifying Bequest of Tangible Property

PART 6. Rules of Construction

Section 2-601. Requirement That Devisee Survive Testator by 120 Hours

Section 2-602. Choice of Law as to Meaning and Effect of Wills

Section 2-603. Rules of Construction and Intention

Section 2-604. Construction That Will Passes All Property: After-Acquired Property

Section 2-605. Anti-lapse; Deceased Devisee; Class Gifts

Section 2-606. Failure of Testamentary Provision

Section 2-607. Change in Securities; Accessions; Nonademption

Section 2-608. Nonademption of Specific Devises in Certain Cases; Sale by Conservator; Unpaid Proceeds of Sale, Condemnation or Insurance

Section 2-609. Non-Exoneration

Section 2-610. Exercise of Power of Appointment

Section 2-611. Construction of Generic Terms to Accord with Relationships as Defined for Intestate Succession

Section 2-612. Ademption by Satisfaction

PART 7. Contractual Arrangements Relating to Death

Section 2-701. Contracts Concerning Succession

PART 8. General Provisions

Section 2-801. Renunciation of Succession

Section 2-802. Effect of Divorce, Annulment and Decree of Separation

Section 2-803. Effect of Homicide on Intestate Succession, Wills, Joint Assets, Life Insurance and Beneficiary Designations

PART 9. Custody and Deposit of Wills

Section 2-901. Deposit of Will With Court in Testator's Lifetime

Section 2-902. Duty of Custodian of Will; Liability

ARTICLE III
Probate of Wills and Administration

PART I. General Provisions

Section 3-101. Devolution of Estate at Death; Restrictions

Section 3-101A. Devolution of Estate at Death; Restrictions

Section 3-102. Necessity of Order of Probate For Will

Section 3-103. Necessity of Appointment For Administration

Section 3-104. Claims Against Decedent; Necessity of Administration

Section 3-105. Proceedings Affecting Devolution and Administration; Jurisdiction of Subject Matter

Section 3-106. Proceedings Within the Exclusive Jurisdiction of Court; Service; Jurisdiction Over Persons

Section 3-107. Scope of Proceedings: Proceedings Independent; Exception

Section 3-108. Probate, Testacy and Appointment Proceedings; Ultimate Time Limit

Section 3-109. Statutes of Limitation on Decedent's Cause of Action

PART 2. Venue for Probate and Administration: Priority to Administer; Demand for Notice

Section 3-201. Venue for First and Subsequent Estate Proceedings; Location of Property

Section 3-202. Appointment or Testacy Proceedings; Conflicting Claim of Domicile in Another State

Section 3-203. Priority Among Persons Seeking Appointment as Personal Representative

Section 3-204. Demand for Notice of Order or Filing Concerning Decedent's Estate

PART 3. Informal Probate and Appointment Proceedings

Section 3-301. Informal Probate or Appointment Proceedings; Application; Contests

Section 3-302. Informal Probate; Duty of Registrar; Effect of Informal Probate

Section 3-303. Informal Probate; Proof and Findings Required

Section 3-304. Informal Probate; Unavailable in Certain Cases

Section 3-305. Informal Probate; Registrar Not Satisfied

Section 3-306. Informal Probate; Notice Requirements

Section 3-307. Informal Appointment proceedings; Delay in Order; Duty of Registrar; Effect of appointment

Section 3-308. Informal Appointment Proceedings; Proof and Findings Required

Section 3-309. Informal Appointment Proceedings; Registrar Not Satisfied

Section 3-310. Informal Appointment Proceedings; Notice Requirements

Section 3-311. Informal Appointment Unavailable in Certain Cases

PART 4. Formal Testacy and Appointment Proceedings

Section 3-401. Formal Testacy Proceedings; Nature; When Commenced

Section 3-402. Formal Testacy or Appointment Proceedings; Petition; Contents

Section 3-403. Formal Testacy Proceedings; Notice of Hearing on Petition

Section 3-404. Formal Testacy Proceedings; Written Objections to Probate

Section 3-405. Formal Testacy Proceedings; Uncontested Cases; Hearings and Proof

Section 3-406. Formal Testacy Proceedings; Contested Cases; Testimony of Attesting Witnesses

Section 3-407. Formal Testacy Proceedings; Burdens in Contested Cases

Section 3-408. Formal Testacy Proceedings; Will Construction; Effect of Final Order in Another Jurisdiction

Section 3-409. Formal Testacy Proceedings; Order; Foreign Will

Section 3-410. Formal Testacy Proceedings; Probate of More Than One Instrument

Section 3-411. Formal Testacy Proceedings; Partial Intestacy

Section 3-412. Formal Testacy Proceeding; Effect of Order; Vacation

Section 3-413. Formal Testacy Proceeding; Vacation of Order For Other Cause

Section 3-414. Formal Proceeding Concerning Appointment of Personal Representative

PART 5. Supervised Administration

Section 3-501. Supervised Administration; Nature of Proceeding

Section 3-502. Supervised Administration; Petition; Order

Section 3-503. Supervised Administration; Effect on Other Proceedings

Section 3-504. Supervised Administration; Powers of Personal Representative

Section 3-505. Supervised Administration; Interim Orders; Distribution and Closing

PART 6. Personal Representative; Appointment, Control and Termination of Authority

Section 3-601. Qualification

Section 3-602. Acceptance of Appointment; Consent to Jurisdiction

Section 3-603. Bond Not Required Without Court Order, Exceptions

Section 3-604. Bond Amount; Security; Procedure; Reduction

Section 3-605. Demand For Bond by Interested Person

Section 3-606. Terms and Conditions of Bonds

Section 3-607. Order Restraining Personal Representative

Section 3-608. Termination of Appointment; General

Section 3-609. Termination of Appointment; Death or Disability

Section 3-610. Termination of Appointment; Voluntary

Section 3-611. Termination of Appointment by Removal; Cause; Procedure

Section 3-612. Termination of Appointment; Change of Testacy Status

Section 3-613. Successor Personal Representative

Section 3-614. Special Administrator; Appointment

Section 3-615. Special Administrator; Who May Be Appointed

Section 3-616. Special Administrator; Appointed Informally; Powers and Duties

Section 3-617. Special Administrator; Formal Proceedings; Power and Duties

Section 3-618. Termination of Appointment; Special Administrator

PART 7. Duties and Powers of Personal Representatives

Section 3-701. Time of Accrual of Duties and Powers

Section 3-702. Priority Among Different Letters

Section 3-703. General Duties; Relation and Liability to Persons Interested in Estate; Standing to Sue

Section 3-704. Personal Representative to Proceed Without Court Order; Exception

Section 3-705. Duty of Personal Representatives; Information to Heirs and Devisees

Section 3-706. Duty of Personal Representative; Inventory and Appraisement

Section 3-707. Employment of Appraisers

Section 3-708. Duty of Personal Representative; Supplementary Inventory

Section 3-709. Duty of Personal Representative; Possession of Estate

Section 3-710. Power to Avoid Transfer

Section 3-711. Powers of Personal Representatives; In General

Section 3-712. Improper Exercise of Power; Breach of Fiduciary Duty

Section 3-713. Sale, Encumbrance or Transaction Involving Conflict of Interest; Voidable; Exceptions

Section 3-714. Persons Dealing with Personal Representative, Protection

Section 3-715. Transactions Authorized for Personal Representatives; Exceptions

Section 3-716. Powers and Duties of Successor Personal Representative

Section 3-717. Co-representatives; When Joint Action Required

Section 3-718. Powers of Surviving Personal Representative

Section 3-719. Compensation of Personal Representative

Section 3-720. Expenses in Estate Litigation

Section 3-721. Proceedings for Review of Employment of Agents and Compensation of Personal Representatives and Employees of Estate

PART 8. Creditors' Claims

Section 3-801. Notice to Creditors

Section 3-802. Statutes of Limitations

Section 3-803. Limitations on Presentation of Claims

Section 3-804. Manner of Presentation of Claims

Section 3-805. Classification of Claims

Section 3-806. Allowance of Claims

Section 3-807. Payment of Claims

Section 3-808. Individual Liability of Personal Representative

Section 3-809. Secured Claims

Section 3-810. Claims Not Due and Contingent or Unliquidated Claims

Section 3-811. Counterclaims

Section 3-812. Execution and Levies Prohibited

Section 3-813. Compromise of Claims

Section 3-814. Encumbered Assets

Section 3-815. Administration in More Than One State; Duty of Personal Representative

Section 3-816. Final Distribution to Domiciliary Representative

PART 9. Special Provisions Relating to Distribution

Section 3-901. Successors' Rights if No Administration

Section 3-902. Distribution; Order in Which Assets Appropriated; Abatement

Section 3-902A. Distribution; Order in Which Assets Appropriated; Abatement

Section 3-903. Right of Retainer

Section 3-904. Interest on General Pecuniary Devise

Section 3-905. Penalty Clause for Contest

Section 3-906. Distribution in Kind; Valuation; Method

Section 3-907. Distribution in Kind; Evidence

Section 3-908. Distribution; Right or Title of Distributee

Section 3-909. Improper Distribution; Liability of Distributee

Section 3-910. Purchasers from Distributees Protected

Section 3-911. Partition for Purpose of Distribution

Section 3-912. Private Agreements Among Successors to Decedent Binding on Personal Representative

Section 3-913. Distributions to Trustee

Section 3-914. Disposition of Unclaimed Assets

Section 3-915. Distribution to Person Under Disability

Section 3-916. Apportionment of Estate Taxes

PART 10. Closing Estates

Section 3-1001. Formal Proceedings Terminating Administration; Testate or Intestate; Order of General Protection

Section 3-1002. Formal Proceedings Terminating Testate Administration; Order Constructing Will Without Adjudicating Testacy

Section 3-1003. Closing Estates: By Sworn Statement of Personal Representative

Section 3-1004. Liability of Distributees to Claimants

Section 3-1005. Limitations on Proceedings Against Personal Representative

Section 3-1006. Limitations on Actions and Proceedings Against Distributees

Section 3-1007. Certificate Discharging Liens Securing Fiduciary Performance

Section 3-1008. Subsequent Administration

PART 11. Compromise of Controversies

Section 3-1101. Effect of Approval of Agreements Involving Trusts, Inalienable Interests, or Interests of Third Persons

Section 3-1102. Procedure for Securing Court Approval of Compromise

PART 12. Collection of Personal Property by Affidavit and Summary Administration; Procedure For Small Estates

Section 3-1201. Collection of Personal Property by Affidavit

Section 3-1202. Effect of Affidavit

Section 3-1203. Small Estates; Summary Administrative Procedure

Section 3-1204. Small Estates: Closing by Sworn Statement of Personal Representative

ARTICLE IV
Foreign Personal Representatives; Ancillary Administration

PART 1. Definitions

Section 4-101. Definitions

PART 2. Powers of Foreign Personal Representatives

Section 4-202. Payment of Debt and Delivery of Property. to Domiciliary Foreign Representative Without Local Administration

Section 4-202. Payment or Delivery Discharges

Section 4-203. Resident Creditor Notice

Section 4-204. Proof of Authority-Bond

Section 4-205. Powers

Section 4-206. Power of Representatives in Transition

Section 4-207. Ancillary and Other Local Administrations; Provisions Governing

PART 3. Jurisdiction Over Foreign Representatives

Section 4-301. Jurisdiction by Act of Foreign Personal Representative

Section 4-302. Jurisdiction by Act of Decedent

Section 4-303. Service on Foreign Personal Representative

PART 4. Judgments and Personal Representative

Section 4-401. Effect of Adjudication for or Against Personal Representative

ARTICLE V
Protection of Persons Under Disability and Their Property

PART 1. General Provisions

Section 5-101. Definitions and Use of Terms

Section 5-102. Jurisdiction of Subject Matter; Consolidation of Proceedings

Section 5-103. Facility of Payment or Delivery

Section 5-104. Delegation of Powers by Parent or Guardian

PART 2. Guardians of Minors

Section 5-201. Status of Guardian of Minor; General

Section 5-202. Testamentary Appointment of Guardian of Minor

Section 5-203. Objection by Minor of Fourteen or Older to Testamentary Appointment

Section 5-204. Court Appointment of Guardian of Minor: Conditions for Appointment

Section 5-205. Court Appointment of Guardian of Minor; Venue

Section 5-206. Court Appointment of Guardian of Minor; Qualifications; Priority of Minor's Nominee

Section 5-207. Court Appointment of Guardian of Minor; Procedure

Section 5-208. Consent to Service by Acceptance of Appointment; Notice

Section 5-209. Powers and Duties of Guardian of Minor

Section 5-210. Termination of Appointment of Guardian; General

Section 5-211. Proceedings Subsequent to Appointment; Venue

Section 5-212. Resignation or Removal Proceedings

PART 3. Guardians of Incapacitated Persons

Section 5-301. Testamentary Appointment of Guardian For Incapacitated Person

Section 5-302. Venue

Section 5-303. Procedure For Court Appointment of a Guardian of an Incapacitated Person

Section 5-304. Findings; Order of Appointment

Section 5-305. Acceptance of Appointment; Consent to Jurisdiction

Section 5-306. Termination of Guardianship for Incapacitated Person

Section 5-307. Removal or Resignation of Guardian; Termination of Incapacity

Section 5-308. Visitor in Guardianship Proceeding

Section 5-309. Notices in Guardianship Proceedings

Section 5-310. Temporary Guardians

Section 5-311. Who May Be Guardian; Priorities

Section 5-312. General Powers and Duties of Guardian

Section 5-313. Proceedings Subsequent to Appointment; Venue

PART 4. Protection of Property of Persons Under Disability and Minors

Section 5-401. Protective Proceedings

Section 5-402. Protective Proceedings; Jurisdiction of Affairs of Protected Persons

Section 5-403. Venue

Section 5-404. Original Petition for Appointment or Protective Order

Section 5-405. Notice

Section 5-406. Protective Proceedings; Request for Notice; Interested Person

Section 5-407. Procedure Concerning Hearing and Order on Original Petition

Section 5-408. Permissible Court Orders

Section 5-409. Protective Arrangements and Single Transactions Authorized

Section 5-410. Who May Be Appointed Conservator; Priorities

Section 5-411. Bond

Section 5-412. Terms and Requirements of Bonds

Section 5-413. Acceptance of Appointment; Consent to Jurisdiction

Section 5-414. Compensation and Expenses

Section 5-415. Death, Resignation or Removal of Conservator

Section 5-416. Petitions for Orders Subsequent to Appointment

Section 5-417. General Duty of Conservator

Section 5-418. Inventory and Records

Section 5-419. Accounts

Section 5-420. Conservators; Title by Appointment

Section 5-421. Recording of Conservator's Letters

Section 5-422. Sale, Encumbrance or Transaction Involving Conflict of Interest, Voidable; Exceptions

Section 5-423. Persons Dealing with Conservators; Protection

Section 5-424. Powers of Conservator in Administration

Section 5-425. Distributive Duties and Powers of Conservator

Section 5-426. Enlargement or Limitation of Powers of Conservator

Section 5-427. Preservation of Estate Plan Claims Against Protected Person; Enforcement

Section 5-428. Individual Liability of Conservator

Section 5-429. Termination of Proceeding

Section 5-430. Payment of Debt and Delivery of Property to Foreign Conservator

Section 5-431. Without Local Proceedings

PART 5. Powers of Attorney

Section 5-501. When Power of Attorney Not Affected by Disability

Section 5-502. Other Powers of Attorney Not Revoked Until Notice of Death or Disability

ARTICLE VI
Non-Probate Transfers

PART 1. Multiple-Party Accounts

Section 6-101. Definitions

Section 6-102. Ownership As Between Parties, and Others; Protection of Financial Institutions

Section 6-103. Ownership During Lifetime

Section 6-104. Right of Survivorship

Section 6-105. Effect of Written Notice to Financial Institution

Section 6-106. Accounts and Transfers Nontestamentary

Section 6-107. Rights of Creditors

Section 6-108. Financial Institution Protection: Payment on Signature of One Party

Section 6-109. Financial Institution Protection; Payment After Death or Disability; Joint Account

Section 6-110. Financial Institution Protection; Payment of P.O.D. Account

Section 6-111. Financial Institution Protection; Payment of Trust Account

Section 6-112. Financial Institution Protection; Discharge

Section 6-113. Financial Institution Protection; Set-off

PART 2. Provisions Relating to Effect of Death

Section 6-201. Provisions for Payment or Transfer at Death

ARTICLE VII
Trust Administration

PART 1. Trust Registration

Section 7-101. Duty to Register Trusts

Section 7-102. Registration Procedures

Section 7-103. Effect of Registration

Section 7-104. Effect of Failure to Register

Section 7-105. Registration, Qualification of Foreign Trustee

PART 2. Jurisdiction of Court Concerning Trusts

Section 7-201. Court; Exclusive Jurisdiction of Trusts

Section 7-202. Trust Proceedings; Venue

Section 7-203. Trust Proceedings; Dismissal of Matters Relating to Foreign Trusts

Section 7-204. Court; Concurrent Jurisdiction of Litigation Involving Trusts and Third Parties

Section 7-205. Proceedings for Review of Employment of Agents and Review of Compensation of Trustee and Employees of Trust

Section 7-206. Trust Proceedings; Initiation by Notice; Necessary Parties

PART 3. Duties and Liabilities of Trustees

Section 7-301. General Duties Not Limited

Section 7-302. Trustee's Standard of Care and Performance

Section 7-303. Duty to Inform and Account to Beneficiaries

Section 7-304. Duty to Provide Bond

Section 7-305. Trustee's Duties; Appropriate Place of Administration; Deviation

Section 7-306. Individual Liability of Trustee to Third Parties

Section 7-307. Limitations on Proceedings Against Trustees After Final Account

ARTICLE VIII
Effective Date and Repealer

Section 8-101. Time of Taking Effect; Provisions for Transition

Section 8-102. Specific Repealer and Amendment

GLOSSARY

Acknowledgement - A formal declaration of one's signature before a notary public.

Actuary - One who computes various insurance and property costs, and calculates the cost of life insurance risks and insurance premiums.

Administrator - One appointed to handle the affairs of a person who has died intestate.

American Arbitration Association (AAA) - National organization of arbitrators from whose panel arbitrators are selected for labor and civil disputes.

American Bar Association (ABA) - A national organization of lawyers and law students.

Assignee - An assignee is a person to whom an assignment is made, also known as a grantee.

Attorney In Fact - An attorney-in-fact is an agent or representative of another given authority to act in that person's name and place pursuant to a document called a "power of attorney."

Beneficiary - A person who is designated to receive property upon the death of another, such as the beneficiary of a life insurance policy, who receives the proceeds upon the death of the insured.

Bequest - Refers to a gift of personal property contained in a will.

Best Evidence Rule - The rule of law which requires the original of a writing, recording or photograph to be produced in order to prove its authenticity.

Capacity - Capacity is the legal qualification concerning the ability of one to understand the nature and effects of one's acts.

Codicil - A document modifying an existing will which, in order to be valid, must be formally drafted and witnessed according to statutory requirements.

Commingle - To combine funds or property into a common fund.

Commingling of Funds - The act of mixing a client's funds with that of a fiduciary, trustee or lawyer's own funds.

Commission - Compensation for services performed which is based on a percentage of an agreed amount.

Common Law - Common law is the system of jurisprudence which originated in England and was later applied in the United States.

Community Property - A form of ownership in a minority of states where a husband and wife are deemed to own property in common, including earnings, each owning an undivided one-half interest in the property.

Conservator - A conservator is the court-appointed custodian of property belonging to a person determined to be unable to properly manage his or her property.

Conveyance - A conveyance is the transfer of property, or title to property, from one person to another, by means of a written instrument and other formalities.

Decedent - A deceased person.

Deed - A legal instrument conveying title to real property.

Duty - The obligation, to which the law will give recognition and effect, to conform to a particular standard of conduct toward another.

Elective Share - Statutory provision that a surviving spouse may choose between taking that which is provided in the spouse's will, or taking a statutorily prescribed share.

Escrow - The arrangement for holding instruments or money which is not to be released until certain specified conditions are met.

Estate - The entirety of one's property, real or personal.

Estate Tax - A tax levied on a decedent's estate in connection with the right to transfer property after death.

Executor - A person appointed by the maker of a will to carry out his or her wishes concerning the administration and distribution of his or estate according to the terms of a will.

Executor's Deed - A deed given by an executor or other fiduciary which conveys real property.

Fiduciary - A fiduciary is a person having a legal duty, created by an undertaking, to act primarily for the benefit of another in matters connected with the undertaking.

Fiscal Year - Any twelve-month period used by a business as its fiscal accounting period.

Fraud - A false representation of a matter of fact, whether by words or by conduct, by false or misleading allegations, or by concealment of that which should have been disclosed, which deceives and is intended to deceive another, and thereby causes injury to that person.

Gift Tax - A tax assessed against the transferor of a gift of property, based upon the fair market value of the property on the date transferred.

Grantee - One who receives a conveyance of real property by deed.

Grantor - One who conveys real property by deed.

Guardian - A person who is entrusted with the management of the property and/or person of another who is incapable, due to age or incapacity, to administer their own affairs.

Heirs - Those individuals who, by law, inherit an estate of an ancestor who dies without a will.

Hereditament - Anything which can be inherited.

Hereditary Succession - The passing of title to an estate according to the laws of descent.

Illegitimate - Illegal or improper. Also used to describe the status of children born out of wedlock.

Illusory Promise - A promise which is unenforceable because its conditions are so indefinite.

Inherit - To take as an heir at law by descent rather than by will.

Inheritance - Property inherited by heirs according to the laws of descent and distribution.

Inheritance Tax - A tax levied on heirs in connection with the right to receive property from a decedent's estate.

Insurance - A contingency agreement, supported by consideration, whereby the insured receives a benefit, e.g. money, in the event the contingency occurs.

Inter Vivos - Latin for "between the living." Refers to transactions made during the lifetime of the parties.

Intestate - The state of dying without having executed a valid will.

Intestate Succession - The manner of disposing of property according to the laws of descent and distribution when the decedent died without leaving a valid will.

Joint Tenancy - The ownership of property by two or more persons who each have an undivided interest in the whole property, with the right of survivorship, whereby upon the death of one joint tenant, the remaining joint tenants assume ownership.

Jurisdiction - The power to hear and determine a case.

Legacy - A gift of personal property by will.

Legatee - One who takes a legacy.

Life Estate - An estate in land held during the term of a specified person's life.

Life Expectancy - The period of time which a person is statistically expected to live, based on such factors as their present age and sex.

Life Insurance - A contract between an insured and an insurer whereby the insurer promises to pay a sum of money upon the death of the insured to his or her designated beneficiary, in return for the periodic payment of money, known as a premium.

Living Trust - A trust which is operated during the life of the creator of the trust.

Marital Property - Property purchased by persons while married to each other.

Minor - A person who has not yet reached the age of legal competence, which is designated as 18 in most states.

Natural Person - A human being as opposed to an artificial "person" such as a corporation.

Net Estate - The gross estate less the decedent's debts, funeral expenses and any other deductions proscribed by law.

Net Income - Gross income less deductions and exemptions proscribed by law.

Net Worth - The difference between one's assets and liabilities.

Pension Plan - A retirement plan established by an employer for the payment of pension benefits to employees upon retirement.

Portfolio - The entirety of one's financial investments.

Power of Attorney - A legal document authorizing another to act on one's behalf.

GLOSSARY

Probate - The process of proving the validity of a will and administering the estate of a decedent.

Referee's Deed - A deed given by a referee or other public officer pursuant to a court order for the sale of property.

Residuary Clause - The clause in a will which conveys to the residuary beneficiaries any property of the testator which was not specifically given to a particular legatee.

Right of Election - In probate law, refers to the right of a surviving spouse to take his or her share of the estate of the deceased either under the terms of the will or as provided by statute.

Right of Survivorship - The automatic succession to the interest of a deceased joint owner in a joint tenancy.

Statute of Limitations - Any law which fixes the time within which parties must take judicial action to enforce rights or thereafter be barred from enforcing them.

Succession - The process by which a decedent's property is distributed, either by will or by the laws of descent and distribution.

Survival Statute - A statute that preserves for a decedent's estate a cause of action for infliction of pain and suffering and related damages suffered up to the moment of death.

Tangible Property - Property which is capable of being possessed, whether real or personal.

Taxable Estate - The decedent's gross estate less applicable statutory estate tax deductions, such as charitable deductions.

Tenancy by the Entirety - A form of ownership available only to a husband and wife whereby they each are deemed to hold title to the whole property, with right of survivorship.

Tenancy in Common - An ownership of real estate by two or more persons, each of whom has an undivided fractional interest in the whole property, without any right of survivorship.

Testator - A male individual who makes and executes a will.

Testatrix - A female individual who makes and executes a will.

Testify - The offering of a statement in a judicial proceeding, under oath and subject to the penalty of perjury.

Testimony - The sworn statement make by a witness in a judicial proceeding.

Title - In property law, denotes ownership and the right to possess real property.

Trust - The transfer of property, real or personal, to the care of a trustee, with the intention that the trustee manage the property on behalf of another person.

Unconscionable - Refers to a bargain so one-sided as to amount to an absence of meaningful choice on the part of one of the parties, together with terms which are unreasonably favorable to the other party.

Undue Influence - The exertion of improper influence upon another for the purpose of destroying that person's free will in carrying out a particular act, such as entering into a contract.

Uniform Gifts to Minors Act (U.G.M.A) - The uniform law adopted by the states providing for a method of making a gift, in trust, to a minor.

Uniform Laws - Laws that have been approved by the Commissioners on Uniform State Laws, and which are proposed to all state legislatures for consideration and adoption.

Verification - The confirmation of the authenticity of a document, such as an affidavit.

Vested - The right to receive, either at present or in the future, a certain benefit, such as a pension from an employer, without further conditions, such as continued employment.

Vitiate - To make void.

Void - Having no legal force or binding effect.

Waiver - An intentional and voluntary surrender of a right.

Ward - A person over whom a guardian is appointed to manage his or her affairs.

Will - A legal document which a person executes setting forth their wishes as to the distribution of their property upon death.

BIBLIOGRAPHY AND ADDITIONAL READING

All-States Wills and Estate Planning Guide. Chicago, IL: American Bar Association, 1995.

Black's Law Dictionary, Fifth Edition . St. Paul, MN: West Publishing Company, 1979.

Bove, Alexander A. *The Complete Book of Wills and Estates.* New York, NY: Henry Holt and Company, 1989.

Ostberg, Kay. *Probate: Settling an Estate: A Step-by-Step Guide, 1990.*

Plotnick, Charles K., Leimberg, Stephan R. *How to Settle an Estate: A Manual for Executors and Trustees.* Yonkers, NY: Consumers Union of the United States, Inc., 1991.

346.7305 JAS
Jasper, Margaret C.
Probate law /
KIN

DISCARD